WHISPERS OF MERCY

For Such a Time as This

SHARED BY LAURA WILCOTT

Trilogy Christian Publishers

A Wholly Owned Subsidiary of Trinity Broadcasting Network

2442 Michelle Drive

Tustin, CA 92780

Copyright © 2024 by Laura Wilcott

Scripture quotations marked amp are taken from the Amplified® Bible (AMP), Copyright © 2015 by The Lockman Foundation. Used by permission. www.Lockman.org. All rights reserved, including the right to reproduce this book or portions thereof in any form whatsoever. Scripture quotations marked kjv are taken from the King James Version of the Bible. Public domain. Scripture quotations marked nasb are taken from the New American Standard Bible® (NASB), Copyright © 1960, 1962, 1963, 1968, 1971, 1972, 1973, 1975, 1977, 1995 by The Lockman Foundation. Used by permission. www.Lockman.org. Scripture quotations marked ncv are taken from the New Century Version®. Copyright © 2005 by Thomas Nelson. Used by permission. All rights reserved. Scripture quotations marked niv are taken from the Holy Bible, New International Version®, NIV®. Copyright © 1973, 1978, 1984, 2011 by Biblica, Inc.TM Used by permission of Zondervan. All rights reserved worldwide. www.zondervan.com. The "NIV" and "New International Version" are trademarks registered in the United States Patent and Trademark Office by Biblica, Inc.TM

For information, address Trilogy Christian Publishing

Rights Department, 2442 Michelle Drive, Tustin, Ca 92780.

Trilogy Christian Publishing/ TBN and colophon are trademarks of Trinity Broadcasting Network.

For information about special discounts for bulk purchases, please contact Trilogy Christian Publishing.

Trilogy Disclaimer: The views and content expressed in this book are those of the author and may not necessarily reflect the views and doctrine of Trilogy Christian Publishing or the Trinity Broadcasting Network.

10 9 8 7 6 5 4 3 2 1

Library of Congress Cataloging-in-Publication Data is available.

ISBN 979-8-89041-571-4

ISBN 979-8-89041-572-1 (ebook)

Acknowledgments

I am immeasurably grateful to my Heavenly Father for my beloved family.

I want to thank my husband, Curtis, daughter, Emily, and son, Garrett, for their generous help at home. Without it, I would never have been able to complete this book.

A special thanks to Brant, my oldest, for all his help compiling these words from my journals.

To Natalie, Shawn, and Jonathan, who are just as much of a blessing in every way:

You are all cherished.

I am so very thankful for the loved ones my Heavenly Father has sent into our lives to be family. You have been faithful in so many ways to water my spirit from a wellspring of love.

Lastly, I want to thank my parents for showing me the love of Jesus—every day of my life.

Preface

Life isn't always easy. Sometimes it is just plain *hard*. We make a mess, we can't get our bearings, we screw things up—sometimes over and over again. We just can't figure it all out. Then, mercifully, God shows up in the thick of it all and begins to rescue us from ourselves. This is exactly what happened to me.

As a teenager, God touched my life so profoundly that I had plenty of zeal, yet I had failed to draw near to Him, and as time went by, I found myself bearing the brunt of a life somewhat disconnected from the Source. But God was merciful and didn't leave me there. He graciously began to show me my need. One day, I asked the Lord to teach me how to be aware of His Presence and how to have a close relationship with Him. My life was so busy, and He seemed to get pushed out of my thoughts way too often. We didn't communicate very well. It was always me doing the talking and never the listening. It didn't seem to me that it was much of a relationship.

I wrote in my spiritual journal about my relationship with the Lord as I saw it: "We don't communicate well enough that I'm aware of what He is saying to me or what to say to Him. I need help!" Soon after, the Lord began to speak, and my behavior seemed to be the topic of discussion—not exactly what I was hoping for. When my child acted out, I would hear, "*You* do that." When he was impatient, wanting everything immediately, I would hear, "*You* do the same thing with Me." When I'd find him on the kitchen counter trying to reach something, I'd say, "Why don't you just *ask* Me?! I can get it much easier." God would whisper, "That's *you*." As uncomfortable as it was for God to keep pointing out my behavior, the behavior itself became an even heavier weight, one I no longer wanted to bear. I desired to cooperate with God but began to see how utterly helpless I seemed to be. As time went by, I began to call out to Him to bring about that change I so desperately desired.

As I was learning to cooperate with God little by little, I would ask Him about things, never really expecting a direct reply—unless it was about my behavior, of course. Then, one day, I asked God what He thought about something and promptly sat down with the Sunday paper and started reading. However, immediately, inside my mind, I heard the words, "Why are you reading the paper? Did you not think I would answer you?"

At first, I dismissed it as my own thoughts. But after some reflection, I realized this question had, in fact, intersected my own thoughts! Therefore, I had to conclude that I could not have initiated the question. I had asked my Heavenly Father something, and He had answered. It was that simple. But I didn't know what to think of it and soon forgot about it, and life went on.

Then, one full year later, I was awakened at exactly 3:00 a.m. and heard God call my name. I got up, and with my journal on my lap, I tried to still the usual whirlwind of thoughts in my head to attempt to listen. Then, suddenly, all the thoughts just stopped—completely. Not one thought was in my head. There was a stillness inside me I had never experienced before. My mind was completely, utterly still, and again, I heard God call my name. I said, "Yes, Lord?" and waited a long time. Then I heard Him call my name again. I'd say, "Yes, Father?" and wait longer still. This went on for a good while... Then, I began to hear Him speak. But this time, more clearly than I ever could have imagined. Morning by morning and always at 3:00 a.m. I would hear that same still, small voice calling my name, and then, as I sat still in His Presence, I'd begin to hear Him whispering ever so gently to my heart. This book is a compilation of more than a dozen journals filled with these conversations.

Table of Contents

Introduction....................xiii	Dive In Without Reserve........ 32
Oh, Such a Lie!................. 1	Making You Stronger 33
The Time for Games Is Over 2	A Work You Will *Not* Believe 34
Met with Empty Hands 3	The Master Craftsman.......... 36
No Right to Interfere 4	Nonsense!..................... 37
Calling a People................. 5	No, It's *Not* Your Imagination 39
The Real Enemy 6	Your Faithful Friend........... 40
For Such a Time as This 7	Man's Approval................. 41
Not as They Suppose............ 9	Leaving Self Behind 42
Just Relax!..................... 10	The Fear of Man............... 43
The Few Who Perceive 11	The One Who Stands Over His Creation...................... 46
Just Cease Your Labor 12	Poised and Ready.............. 47
Even a Donkey 13	Elusive Is the Kingdom 49
In My Kingdom Now........... 14	Indistinguishable to the Untrained Eye.................. 50
Pasture of Rest................. 15	We're Moving Forward!......... 51
Turn It Off.................... 17	Out of the Dust................ 52
Dressed in Royal Robes......... 18	Eyes Wide Open............... 53
Fine Tuned.................... 19	In a Place Called Blessed 55
Only Triumph................. 20	Filtering Out the Noise 56
At the Master's Table 22	Busy, Busy, Busy............... 57
They Have Forgotten........... 23	Nothing Reserved.............. 58
Fashioned for a Purpose 25	They Have Left................ 59
Tried in the Fire 27	Only Tasted, Barely Touched 60
The Shadow of the Enemy....... 28	Upward, Higher, Closer......... 61
A Pawn in My Hand............ 29	Bought with a Price 63
A Voice Behind You 31	

In the Hull of the Boat 64	As the Clouds Full of Rain. 97
Emptied Out, Only to Be Filled . . 65	Those Precious Few 98
Into My Fire. 66	Seize the Moment! 99
I Work Alone! 67	Your Ever-Present Help 100
No Better Time 68	To Be Deposited 101
Starving 69	Where Will It End? 102
Seekers of My Kingdom. 71	Holding On, Missing Out 103
Your Very Great Reward 72	Get Your Running Shoes On 105
Run from It! 73	In God's Pickup Truck 106
A Higher Dimension 74	Close Beside You. 107
What Tender Care, What Loving Kindness! 75	Praise Stills the Avenger. 108
	There Is No Other 109
My Finished Work 77	What It's All About. 111
My Desire 78	Not as a Mere Reflection 112
Molded for This Hour 80	Just Love Them. 114
Move Over. 81	That Secret Place 115
Beyond Their Eyes, Into My Realm 82	Met by the Living God. 116
	Isn't It Enough? 118
Only to Be Carried 84	At Arm's Length 120
The Vastness, the Immensity. 85	Step Into Your Calling 122
So Much Better 86	Their "Holy" Ambitions. 124
Trivial Pursuits 87	Blindfolded 128
They Come Close with Their Lips 89	An Awesome Work. 129
	That Gentle Nudge 130
He Will Be Evicted. 90	What Patience! What Love! 132
Many Enlisted 91	As Fast as You Can Listen 134
Jump into This River! 92	Out of Your Comfort Zone 135
Drink Deeply. 93	*I'm* the Gift! 136
Have Another Helping! 94	Illusions of Control. 138
Strategically Placed. 95	

The Whys of Life 139	As One Who Commands an Army 172
The Picture Many Paint of Me . . 140	Begin to Reign! 173
Carried Swiftly 142	Not by Might, Nor by Power. . . . 174
The Voice of the Accuser 143	The Lovers' Path. 175
Remember 144	Robbed of Precious Moments. . . 177
His Awesome Plans 145	Just What the Enemy Wants 178
Surpassing Man's Ability to Reason 147	An Awesome Task at Hand 179
The Potter, Not the Clay 148	Stand Up! Say "No!" 181
As a Man Who Guards a City . . . 149	This Isn't McDonalds! 182
Driving a Wedge 150	Fall on Me 184
As a Treasure to Be Guarded 151	A Sweet Place 185
Mapped Out Carefully 152	A Work Birthed in Them. 187
I AM Tomorrow 153	Created to Soar 188
Jars of Clay 155	As the Air They Breathe 189
Mercy on Them All 156	Hovering over the Ground 192
In the Midst of Despair 157	This Foolish Generation 193
"Not My Will but Thine!" 158	In a Smoke-Filled Room 194
That Spark, That Fire, That Blaze 159	Staggering Under the Weight. . . . 196
Just Whisper My Name 160	Take a Deep Breath 197
Your Partner, Your Lover, Your Friend 161	On the Very Edge 198
See Me as I AM. 163	Where Fear Is but a Memory . . . 199
To Quench a Thirst 164	The Benefit of Doing It My Way 200
Be Aflame! 165	As a Picture Painted on a Wall . . 201
Enjoy the Ride 166	What a Mess!. 202
Where You Veered Off 167	A Deep Reservoir 204
Taking Possession 168	Dear to Me. 205
Religious Fantasies 170	Make Up Your Mind. 206

XI

Quit Playing God!............207	Stumbling Around in the Dark..................241
My Bride 209	Speak That Precious Message...244
Much More to Come 210	Don't Shut Up That River 245
Shout It If You Have To 211	Yes, I AM *That* Good..........246
Right at Your Feet.............212	My Jewel, Placed as I See Fit....247
Prevailing to the Point of Peace..213	Woven for This Time in History....................248
Running Around on Empty.....214	Get Off Your Agenda 249
Give Out from the Well 215	The Secret Things of My Kingdom.................250
Love Them Gently 217	Called Up, Sent Out 253
The Wrong Frequency.........218	Handcrafted for My Glory......254
As the Waves Begin to Rise.....220	Empowered for This Hour 255
Carry Them If You Have To 221	Nothing Except Their Heart....257
That Door of Love 222	Take the Exit! 259
It Tastes No Different..........223	Handpicked for This Moment...260
Beyond What You Can Imagine .224	As I Bear Them Up on My Wings 261
Clouded by Wants 226	Endnotes 263
The Higher Realm 227	
No Longer Speaking for the Enemy!.................228	
The *Real* Happenings..........229	
Of Nothing Are You More Sure .230	
A Path Swept Clean 231	
Vast, Explosive, Dynamic 232	
Stand in the Gap! 234	
More than Enough 235	
That Entrance of Peace 236	
Throw Off Those Grave Clothes!238	
A Gathering of the Camps......239	
Eating Hotdogs in the Stands ...240	

Introduction

Do you sense God is trying to get your attention? Does it seem that something new is happening in you? Maybe you have always thought you were in control of your life, but now it seems your spiritual journey is being orchestrated by the Father.

Are you seeing your motives more clearly? Is the Spirit of God nudging you in a new direction toward Him? Is He showing you that He is in charge, not you? Well, you are not alone. The temptation is to say, "Nothing is new. Everything is as it has always been," but God spoke through the prophet Isaiah, saying, "See, I am doing a new thing. Now, it springs up. Do you not perceive it?"[1]

The very nature of the dawn is that it is *new*. The very nature of the sunrise is that it ushers in a *new* day. Amazingly, Peter the Apostle wrote the following words, not to those who didn't know Him but to believers—to those who already knew Christ as their Savior, "And we heard this voice which came from heaven... and so we have the prophetic word confirmed, which you do well to heed as a light that shines in a dark place *until the day dawns and the morning star rises in your hearts.*"[2]

Perhaps the very thing that is happening in you is the stirring of the Spirit of God. Perhaps He is waking you up from a spiritual slumber. Perhaps all is not as you had imagined. Maybe there is more—much, much more!

For the Father to give a fresh glimpse into His heart is grace—undeniably.

For Him to open up our minds and our ears to hear is mercy—unquestionably.

Will you enter in with me? Will you sit at His feet and rest with me for a while? As you open the pages of this book, breathe in deeply, beloved.

He is here.

Oh, Such a Lie!

Take a good look at where you've been. Examine closely where you are now and see if My hand has not fashioned you thus far. I've taken you from a heap and molded you to be a vessel as I see fit.

I'm not through! I'm still at work! I haven't slowed down or given up!

> I'm busy about what I'm doing.
>
> I'm attentive to every detail.
>
> I HAVE A PLAN!

So many believe I've given up on them and am gone. *Oh, if they only knew of My tender mercies, they would not believe such a lie!* I long for My people to see My hand in their lives, to see the wind of My Spirit blow on them.

They miss Me. They cannot see. They are blind to My work. They are deaf to My call.

> OH, THAT THEY WOULD OPEN THEIR EYES AND LOOK UNTIL THEY SEE, THAT THEY WOULD OPEN THEIR EARS AND LISTEN UNTIL THEY HEAR!

The Time for Games Is Over

Get to work. *You've been drafted. You are a purchased possession.* This is not the time for games. When the Spirit speaks, give attention!

> Don't pass over My direction.
>
> Don't neglect My instruction.
>
> Be quick to obey!

It's time to begin walking circumspectly, not turning to the right or to the left. The hour has come for you to order your conversations aright, to give thought to your every action, your every thought.

> I want to train you.
>
> You must test everything.
>
> I will lead you step by step.

Keep your eyes fixed directly before you. Keep your eyes on the goal *for the prize of the upward call of God.*[3]

> You are in active service.
>
> The time for games is over!

Met with Empty Hands

Oh, I would that we would stroll through My garden unencumbered by your desires! My plans for you are so much better than any plan you could ever have.

Wait.

Rest.

For all that I have for you, all that is waiting at the door must be met with empty hands. You must shed everything to go through My door, to walk into My blessings.

> *[In my mind's eye I saw someone wearing several layers of old dirty ragged clothes and an old coat carrying a suitcase standing at a door with Jesus and all His blessings on the other side.]*

They must shed everything. No one enters into My bounty, into My rich blessing, any other way.

Let go!

Let go of your bundle of desires.

No Right to Interfere

You have no right to stand in the way of My Word to someone. You have no right to interfere in the message I have for one of My children.

> You must obey.

> You must be a faithful messenger.

> You must be faithful.

I'll tell you what to say. Don't add anything to it—ever, not even your thoughts. I'm going to begin to draw many into the same obedience. *You need to lead the way.*

The time has not yet come for some to see the Kingdom, but you will see it, so don't be astonished at the things I'm doing.

> Just follow Me.

> Just seek My Face.

> I will lead you if you follow Me.

The hour has come for men to see Me in all My Glory, Me in all My splendor. They will not obey, but they will see.

Calling a People

You must begin to flow as I carry you. Don't hold back in fear.

Am I not faithful?

I will make it plain to you what you are to do. Oh, the time is short! For My plan is to call a people out of the world, which is in the churches.

I'm calling a people to holiness, to hear My voice, to call on My Name, to seek My Face.

You are one who must hear. You must learn to be still. Be quick to hear Me. Be quick to obey, knowing that I AM faithful.

Learn My Word.

Let Me teach you.

Let Me open up the Scriptures to you.

In them, there is Life, the Life that you are to speak. I've called you by My Name. You are to be a light in a dark place.

The Real Enemy

He's not worth mentioning his name. I will not give My Glory to another. It is shameful what My people will give to the devil. He has nothing that I have not commanded. He is not to blame for much of man's suffering when they are drawn away by their own lusts and enticed.

My people must *cast down the vain imaginations and bring every thought into captivity to the obedience of Christ.*[4] They have not done this. Many are blind to who the real enemy is. The flesh wars against the soul.

Bring every thought into captivity. Let Me be Lord over your mind.

Renew your mind.

Your mind is too full. *Wash it out!* Your thinking takes up My time. Your plans, your ideas, I don't need them, so wash them out!

[**"How do I do it, Lord?" I asked.**]

Your ears will hear a voice behind you saying, "This is the way, walk in it."[5]

For Such a Time as This

Don't be concerned with how I will perform My Word I speak in your ear. *Just stand and walk.* You will see. You will not be disappointed. You will not be dismayed. For haven't I said, "Fear not for I AM with you. Be not dismayed for I AM your God. I will strengthen you. Yes, I will help you. I will uphold you with the right hand of My righteousness."[6]

It is My righteous right hand that carries out every detail of My Word spoken in season, every command issued, every decree proclaimed, every prophecy foretold, every promise given.

So, stand tall when you speak! Don't be bowed down!

Speak as the oracles of God![7]

Speak with all confidence! Speak with authority! For I have raised you up for this hour—for such a time as this!

Speak only what you hear Me speaking and do only what you see Me doing.

Not as They Suppose

["Lord, please don't shut me off," I cried.]

I haven't shut you off. My mercies are new every morning. Great is My faithfulness. You just don't know Me well enough.

Taste and see that the Lord is good![8]

It is He that has made you, and not you, yourselves. You are the sheep of His pasture. The Good Shepherd cares for the sheep. He toils tirelessly to keep them in the fold. You are of His fold. You are protected.

You will see things others have not seen. Others have looked to an image of Me that is not reality.

I AM not as they suppose.

I AM gentle, merciful, and kind. I do not afflict willingly. I gently hold them in My hand as you should with yours.

I wait patiently for them to grow in their knowledge of Me. Only this knowledge sets man free from worry and strain to perform, to yield results as man would have them do.

Just Relax!

I AM the Vine. You are the branches. Apart from Me you can do nothing.[9]

So wait. Wait on the Lord.

He is your deliverer, your advocate, your friend.

He has a plan for you, a course set before time for you to walk. He will perform it. So wait. *Do not be like those who walk in their own power.*

They fail.

They are deceived.

Their self-righteous acts I abhor.

You must look to Me. I have you in the palm of My hand.

Just relax and let Me do the work.

Only what I do will remain. Only what I do will produce the fruit that will remain. You must see that all that I do is in a set order to cause growth, definite and determined, to produce fruit for Eternal Life.

The Few Who Perceive

You will not be ruled by your mind any longer. Those days are over. You must be ruled by My Spirit. Set your face like a flint to catch the wave of My Spirit as one does on the sea. I will hold you up. I will set you upright so that you will not topple.

> Just listen to Me.
>
> Don't be too busy to listen.

I want to be the Lord of your day, the Light on your path, so acknowledge Me in all your ways, and I will direct your paths.

> Seek My Face.

I do not wish to withhold from My children. You will hear and perceive things not perceived thus far by the many but only by the few.

> Take your stand among those who hearken unto My voice. I do have the few who perceive My comings and goings, My ways among men.

They have learned to hearken unto My voice. They stop, they wait, they listen while the worldly church sets a course without direction—without hearing My voice.

Just Cease Your Labor

As a baby nurses at the breast, so My children remain. They will not be weaned. They refuse to accept My instruction, correction, or direction.

They set a course in the dark. They stumble, they fall, but I long to clear their way if they would but let go and be carried. They try to climb a mountain not set out for them. I will make their paths straight as they call out to Me.

I AM their Source.

If they would but realize this, they would be free. Pray for their eyes to be opened. This is not the time to look back but to press on to maturity.

Rest in Me.

Enter that rest that I have for you.[10]

Just stop working.

You don't have to work at resting; just cease your labor.

Even a Donkey

Stop looking at yourself. You are not the focus. Can a water pot bring relief? No!

> ## Stop saying, "Why me?" Start saying, "Yes, Lord!"

You will be faithful, but you must step out of the way. If the focus is on you, you will be overwhelmed. You are only the vessel, not the Life-giving water.

My plan will go on. It is *My* work. It is *My* workings in you. Do not be consumed with yourself. I can use anyone, *even a donkey*.[11] That is how *men* think—they focus on the vessel, but *I* will be glorified.

My purposes will stand with or without you, but you will be a voice of encouragement. Men will long for it. Men will cry out for relief in times of trouble. My water will bring the relief they seek, but I need a vessel. My vessels of Life, My vessels of mercy are part of the plan, so don't be overwhelmed, but look at Me and My workings. They are not yours, so don't be troubled. I have a plan.

Stand. Don't waver, for I am ready to bring you into maturity. You may think that where you are in life is discouraging, but I have made it such to prepare you for the times ahead.

Keep your head up. Keep your focus fixed on Me. I love you and have so many workings to work.

Oh, My child, let Me teach you My ways!

In My Kingdom Now

Nothing is as it seems to the senses. You cannot go by your senses. They will fool you. A spiritual message must be spiritually discerned. Don't make assumptions. Use your spiritual ears. *If anyone has ears to hear, let him hear.*[12]

Stop saying, "I can't do it!" Of course, you can't. Of course, you need Me.

Speak My words! Speak Life!

I want to do new things in you and through you. Don't look back—ever!

You are in My Kingdom now, ruled by My rules. Everything is different in My Kingdom. I said, *"Thy kingdom come..."*[13] The Kingdom is in you, not to be perceived by natural means.

Don't live by natural means.

Live by that which is spiritual.

The laws are different. The Spirit searches the deep things of God.

The natural misses God completely.

Pasture of Rest

My pastures are empty. My sheep do not hear My voice. They do not follow Me. They have forsaken the Way of Righteousness. They have turned to a dark, slippery path. They cannot see. They cannot hear. They refuse the voice of the Shepherd. They are like stubborn mules.

> Oh, that they would hear My tender callings wooing them to come and feed, wooing them to the waters!

I would nurse them. I would teach them to stand if they would but heed My voice. A gentle hand will lead them.

There are a few who follow Me through rocky places who trust Me to lead them the right way. They see the spacious place, a place of rest, a place of feeding, a secure place. My loving hand will guide them to a pasture of rest.

Their toil will end. They will cease their labors while the others wander in darkness. Distress and anguish await them. They stumble on the path. I will teach them the way, but their lessons will be hard.

There will be no rest for the weary, only a fearful expectation of judgment in the fire of My Presence. I will burn away the chaff. They will be left but not full. They will be lacking. They will be filled, but only through hardships. A long and arduous path awaits them if they fail to follow Me.

I WOULD HAVE MY CHILDREN COME AND DRINK, TO ABIDE IN THE SHELTER OF MY WINGS, TO REST IN THE SHADOW OF MY PRESENCE. I DRAW THEM TO ME.

Turn It Off

Now is the time for you to start setting some things in order. Stop listening with your mind. It's not reliable. Only your spirit is able to discern what I am saying.

> **Turn your mind off.**
>
> **Shut it down.**

For only then will you be able to hear correctly.

I want to be a fountain of Life to you, a fountain in which you laugh and rejoice, a fountain to quench your thirst to wash the mire away, to refresh, to renew, to replenish your spirit.

> OH, COME TO MY FOUNTAIN AND DRINK!
>
> TASTE OF THE WATERS OF LIFE!

There is so much more for you, so much I hold in My hand, longing to shower on you!

[*"How do I experience more of you?"* I inquired.]

> **Turn off your mind.**
>
> **Let your spirit rule.**

Only your spirit can grasp the Kingdom realm.

Dressed in Royal Robes

Begin to walk in My Kingdom as royalty. You are dressed in royal robes. Don't stoop on the side of the road. My Kingdom awaits for My sons and daughters to reign. Their position is ready. Their robes are fitted. But their throne is empty.

They must take their stand. I, the King of kings, await—await for My children to run to Me! I want to seat them in high places with Me. Their throne has been prepared from the foundation of the world. They will rule, they will reign, but only as they yield to My Spirit.

I have a work to work in them—an urgent work. They are so busy working but not My works, speaking but not My words. They are deceived. They are enslaved to preoccupation. It strangles them. It chokes My Word so that it is unfruitful. They are too busy for Me.

> I WOULD THAT THEY WOULD SHED THEIR CLOTHING AND JUMP INTO MY FOUNTAIN OF LIFE-GIVING WATER. I WOULD THAT THEY WOULD TOSS AWAY THEIR FILTHY RAGS AND DIVE INTO MY WATERS. ALL THEIR RIGHTEOUS ACTS ARE AS FILTHY RAGS TO ME.[14]

Today is a new day, a day to walk uprightly, not stooping off My way. Turn your attention to My Spirit. Turn your eyes upon Me.

Shared by Laura Wilcott

Fine Tuned

I want to fine-tune My children to My frequency, the children I have purchased out of the world to serve Me. They hear static because they haven't been ready.

You need to heed My warnings to protect the words I give you. You must be faithful with the treasures entrusted to you. They must be handled correctly.

You do not have the right to tell anyone anything I say unless I tell you to. You have no right to keep a message to yourself that is for someone else, either. You must learn not to assume what needs to be said or done in a particular situation. You need to stop and listen.

Ask of Me and see if I will not make a way in the wilderness. Wait and see. See if I will not set in order the things that must take place to propel you into the service to which you have been called.

No one can stand in your way. Let no one dissuade you from taking what has been placed before you. Let no one stand between you and your destiny. Let no one break your fellowship with Me.

You must stand to take the mantle I have for you. You will go forward. You will continue in the path laid out before you. You will set your face like a flint. You will not falter. You will not fail. For I AM behind you to make you stand, to make you take hold of that for which I took hold of you.

Only Triumph

Only success awaits you. Only triumph awaits you in the way. As one who stands in triumph over his foes, so you will stand in triumph over the ones who would stand in your way. For I have a set course, a sure course for your feet to follow.

You will not stumble in the way as you keep your gaze set directly before you. Trust Me, for I will show you things to come. You must trust Me, for I will lead you on a sure path, but it will be hard.

Few will follow along the same way, for they will see the difficulty of the path and will turn back, but your eyes will fix on Me.

You will not be moved.

You will seek only My will.

You will hear only My counsel.

No other will you follow, not even fear, for you know of My goodness. You know of My faithfulness; thus, you will not turn back.

Though some will endeavor to correct you while others mock, you will place one foot in front of the other, continuing on the course laid out before you. Their taunts and jeers will only make you stronger. Their whispers will only make you more resolute.

My objective will be your objective, My agenda, yours, as you see the Kingdom unfold before you, as your vision gets clearer and clearer. *Watch and see.*

At the Master's Table

Take your stand, for I am about to make you, bend you, mold you into a vessel fit for My use. You will be placed at the Master's table to be used as He desires to be poured out for the many.

You will be a refreshing stream for a thirsty land, a well of water for a tired soul. Drink of the water of Life, for you have much to give out in the coming days. Drink and quench your thirst, for I AM the Life-giving water. Drink of Me, for I will fill you up.

I AM *EVERYTHING* YOU NEED.

Come to Me. Wash yourself. Be refreshed for the journey ahead. Learn to drink of My water. Learn to wash in the river of Life. My water quenches every thirst.

DRINK AND BE THIRSTY NO MORE.

Partake of Me. Let My fountain flow over you. Let Me wash away all that you were. For in Me, you are complete. Only in Me are you made whole.

Rest in My arms of love, for I have taken hold of you. My child, you are safe right where you are. Only in Me will you find rest from your labors, your constant striving to please man and self.

Rest in My work. Please only Me.

FOR I AM THE KEEPER OF YOUR SOUL.

Shared by Laura Wilcott

They Have Forgotten

I AM the only One who can broaden your way before you. Man cannot see the road, its winding and turning, its dangers and obstacles, but I see all and am well able to see you through, so trust Me.

> Listen to Me, not man.
>
> I will not lead you astray.
>
> I will keep you to the course.

Don't listen to the nonsense some will speak. You will know My voice. Do not give them your attention.

Please only Me. For the path that I lead you down will be a path of Life. For those who will follow will see Me in all My Glory. My Glory will light the way. I will make the way light before you. Your steps will be made in the light. I do not desire for My children to stumble in darkness.

> THEY LOSE THEIR WAY BECAUSE THE LIGHT OF MY FAITHFULNESS THEY HAVE FORGOTTEN. THE LAMP OF CORRECTION THEY DO NOT HEED.

My Word is a lamp unto your feet, a light unto your path.[15] Trust My Word. I will not lead you astray.

Do not step into darkness. Wait for My Light to show the path.

Do not venture ahead. Do not lag behind.

I will set the pace. You will be able to follow, for I will make you able. *Now cast all your anxiety on Me, for I care for you.*[16]

Fashioned for a Purpose

Can a jewel say to a jeweler, "Place me here. Put me there"? Yet I have placed you, and you say, "Why?" Why is the bird asked to fly? Why is the eagle asked to soar? Are they not fashioned for that purpose? Are they not created for that very thing?

Take up the wings that I have given you.

Don't stay in the nest.

Don't hide in the shadows.

There is a reason you see what you see. I do not ask of you anything that I will not undergird you. I will be as the mother hawk.

I will not let you fall. Rely on Me.

[*On two separate occasions, I saw mother hawks teaching their sets of babies to fly. Each mother flew under one baby and bopped him up in the air with one wing, then flew under the other and did the same with the other wing. I was thinking about what I had seen as He spoke to my heart.*]

LET GO AND BE CARRIED.

Tried in the Fire

You have an enemy. He seeks to destroy My works but cannot. I will prevail. You must recognize the enemy. *Cast down vain imaginations and every high thing that exalts itself against the knowledge of God, bringing every thought into captivity to the obedience of Christ.*[17]

My people are destroyed for lack of knowledge.[18] They wander about seeking in vain the pleasure they desire. They covet but cannot get their desires fulfilled. They're insatiable.

> **They don't want Me, the Author of life—only what I can give them.**

Oh, that they would see My hand extended toward them! Oh, that they would walk in the path laid out for them! *My yoke is easy, and My burden is light,*[19] but they have chosen the hard way. My will will be done. My plans will not be thwarted, yet they have chosen the difficult road. They have not taken My hand. I AM gentle. My road is easy.

My hand will lead them down a path not forged for them because of their stubborn, unrepentant hearts. They will be tested and tried in the furnace of affliction. My furnace is hot and melts away the dross. I want to take the dross out of you. I want to refine you as gold is refined, as silver is tried in the fire.

The Shadow of the Enemy

You must stand against the wiles of the wicked one. You must *resist him*[20] firm in the faith. He will not prevail as you stand firm, not giving in for a moment. Do not play his game. Cheap and petty are his tricks.

You must recognize them.

He uses selfishness and pride, arrogance and haughtiness to do his work. Recognize these and resist him firm in the faith. Do not let him get a foothold, for *you are bought with a price.*[21]

You are My instrument designed to carry out My plans, which will stand. They will stand as My people hearken unto My voice and resist the evil one, knowing that I AM the King of Heaven not to be toyed with.

You must learn to recognize the shadow of the enemy as it lurks about. You must learn to detect his workings. He seeks to destroy you, but I will destroy him. His days are numbered.

He will not see victory.

His children are fleeting. They will not see victory. Their works will be destroyed, burned up in the fire.

A Pawn in My Hand

You must know the enemy: his schemes, his tactics, his lies. He is a liar, *the father of all lies*.[22] You must realize this, for he uses it to his advantage. He is a deceiver leading My people along the wrong path. He blinds their eyes to the truth. *My truth sets men free*,[23] free from worldly lusts and fears. They do not walk in their freedom because they have believed a lie.

> Recognize the enemy.
>
> Deal with him.

Do not succumb to evil desires that plague you. Do not give in to them for a moment.

> Resist immediately.
>
> Test everything.

For My work will be your focus. You will not be distracted. You will not be dissuaded, for My purposes will stand, for I have already gained the victory.

There is no other outcome. He knows he is defeated. Know the Power that is at your disposal. Know the awesome Power that is at your command. For My Word is powerful, *able to quench the fiery darts of the wicked one*,[24] able to extinguish his plans. He does not have a voice but what I give him. He does not have an audience but what I lay at his feet. He works My works for a purpose.

He carries out the plan set for him for *My glory*. He can do no other. He is a pawn in My hand, played out as I see fit.

You are under My command.

A Voice Behind You

Yours is a road not traveled often. Keep to the path set out for you. Don't look behind and don't look ahead, for today is the day of salvation. Your ears will hear a voice behind you saying, "This is the way. Walk in it." Be careful to tread the path I set out for you and not another.

Don't be anxious on the way. Don't fret or be concerned with what others may think.

> YOU ARE CALLED TO FULFILL A PLAN LAID OUT FOR *YOU*, NOT ANOTHER, SO DON'T LOOK TO MAN FOR APPROVAL. LOOK TO ME.

I AM the One who determines the course of your life, and it's a sure course, one of trials and yet success.

> REST IN MY PLAN, FOR I HAVE YOUR BEST INTEREST AT HEART.

I can see the road ahead, so you must trust Me to guide you in the way I see fit. It may seem hard. It may seem long. But time will show that My way was the right way and My plan absolutely necessary for your growth.

> REST IN MY GOODNESS, IN MY LOVING-KINDNESS.
>
> REST IN MY TENDER CARE.

Dive In Without Reserve

You have not seen the full extent of My mercies toward you. You have not dived into My arms without reserve.

Can I not be trusted?

Am I a faithless father who would abandon His children to their own devices to their own childish ways? No, I will instruct, I will rebuke, and I will train My children to obey.

I AM not a faithless father who will leave you where you are even if you do not understand My workings, even if you question Me. For I AM faithful to perfect you and present you blameless before Me by the means that I choose by the path that I have chosen for you to follow.

Don't question My goodness, for I AM good. Don't question My faithfulness, for I AM faithful. Don't question My ability to keep you, for I AM the One who holds your hand.

I have kept you all along the way.

Making You Stronger

You could not stand if it were not for Me and My mercies. For My mercies have been abundant toward you, My grace ever by your side.

>Trust Me. Hold tight to Me.

>Cleave to Me.

>For I AM your Hiding Place.

You need not worry about tomorrow, for I have all your tomorrows in My hand. You needn't worry about today, for I am well able to see you through the difficulties designed for the very purpose of making you stronger.

I do nothing but for a purpose, and My purposes will stand—not for *your* glory, but *Mine*. You can only do what I have established for you, so abandon yourself to Me.

>I will carry you.

>I will see you through.

The road ahead is so filled with triumph, not as you have planned, but according to My plans, for My plans are not as your plans.

A Work You Will Not Believe

Oh, that you would rest in My plans for you! I will begin to unfold them in the coming days. You will be incredulous, not knowing the full extent of My goodness, not perceiving the full extent of My loving kindness toward you, for your vision is shortsighted and blurred.

> You have not seen or understood fully the thoughts I think toward you, or you would have abandoned yourself to Me long ago.

Trust in My goodness, for in Me is all the success you desire, yet it will not be as you suppose.

You see in the natural, and My Kingdom is not in the natural. You see in the natural, yet it cannot be perceived with your senses. Wait on Me, for I will come. I am coming to do a work in you that you will not believe.

Only wait.

Be still.

Yes, be still.

Shared by Laura Wilcott

[*Will you talk to me, Lord?*]

NOT ONLY WILL I TALK WITH YOU, I'LL POUR MY HEART OUT TO YOU. I AM READY TO REVEAL MY HEART TO YOU. IT IS NOT A QUESTION AS TO WHETHER *I* AM READY BUT *YOU*.

The Master Craftsman

Now that you have delved into some of My workings, do not think you know anything. Do not presume to have laid hold of Me, for My workings far exceed your ability to fathom even the smallest work that I work.

You can know nothing unless it is granted to you. You can do nothing unless it is so ordained, so empty yourself into Me.

> GATHER UP THE FRAGMENTS I HAVE GIVEN YOU AND WAIT FOR ME TO FORM THEM INTO A MASTERPIECE, PIECE BY PIECE, AS I SEE FIT.

I will take what I give you and create out of it a creation for My glory.

ONLY WAIT ON ME.

Any work you work will be in vain. You needn't say, "Work your work in me," for I am already doing My work and will continue until Christ is formed in you.

Relax.

Rest.

Be still.

Don't get caught up in your busy schedule so much so that you fail to rest. Throw yourself onto Me every moment.

Nonsense!

Because I love you, I will not leave you the way you are. My creation, My offspring, must rise above those feelings of despair, for I have ordained that they walk a road of misery for a season along the journey. Those feelings of inadequacy are absolutely necessary, for man is inadequate and must come to that realization.

How can an archer who practices night and day know he will hit the target if the arrow is made by an untrustworthy man? Yet My people believe that their lives are orchestrated in part by the devil.

They say, "The devil this and the devil that." Well, I say, "Hogwash!" The devil isn't orchestrating anything. He didn't take over My plan. He didn't circumvent My workings. He hasn't barged into My party. Nonsense!

I AM at the center of everything, and you say, "How can this be? I've seen the atrocities!" Yes, oh yes, I must turn My head at some of the things man does, but I have created man to be so vile.

Only in his wicked state will he ever truly see God. For as his eyes are opened, he sees how indescribably awesome is *the Love of God*,[25] how inexplicably amazing is His grace, a grace that reaches down into man's desperately wicked state and *redeems him in His Love*.[26] Man cannot fathom how I work. Man cannot conceive of My plan.

You say, "What about collateral damage? What about those along the way who suffer at the hands of such wickedness?" I say, "Those servants of Mine that have been set in that place could never know the depth of My Love and the abundance of

My Power to heal and restore if they had not walked that road of despair of bitter heartbreak."

You say, "It can't be, surely not!" Oh yes, and more! How will anyone know of My pain in redeeming them if they have felt none? How will man see My heart if they haven't walked through grief? For I grieved once! I was in pain! *I suffered loss for all mankind.*[27]

No. Only by My road that I have laid out will man ever truly know Me as I AM. Yes, it seems inconceivable. Oh, we'd love to blame the devil for what we see, but *man's heart is desperately wicked; who can know it?*[28] I have just restrained the many from themselves!

No, It's *Not* Your Imagination

Is it so puzzling that I would speak in such a way to your heart? Is it so astonishing that I would choose to speak clearly, directly to your spirit? *Can I not speak any way I choose?* Why would I speak through riddles when I have your heart and your full attention?

So many believe I am hiding Myself when I am not. When they hear My voice in their ear, they say, "It can't be. Surely not!"

> They rationalize away My sweet callings. They brush aside My gentle voice, thinking all the while they've imagined it.

They are so wrapped up in themselves that they think it's their own thoughts, their own imaginations saying what they want to hear, yet it is I who speaks to their heart, who whispers in their ear.

> Oh, that My people would acknowledge Me and come close when I call!

Your Faithful Friend

Consider the times I've held you. Consider the times I've picked you up and dusted you off. Consider the times I've come searching for you when you've wandered off. Now consider My grace, for it is this grace that keeps you. It is My goodness that follows you and goes before you.

In the coming days, you must call to mind My grace and My goodness, for the work that I will do, My expedient work, will seem harsh and difficult to bear, but as you center up into Me as you recall My goodness and grace, you will rest.

Let Me be your all in all.

Let Me be your faithful friend.

Oh, I AM so much bigger than what you could ever face. I'm so much better than you could ever think. I'm so much stronger than you can conceive.

I'm higher than your thoughts can take you, deeper than you can go. I'm stronger than any storm and deeper than any valley. I'm there when you close your eyes at night and at the dawn of each new day.

Oh, see My rich bounty. See My precious treasure at your feet.

Man's Approval

Cease your preoccupation with what man thinks. You are not here to please man. Do not give any attention to the deceptiveness of the exterior. From now on, I want you to cast your cares onto Me and walk in My realm.

When you walk by the Spirit, keeping your focus directly on Me, you will not be overcome by the anxieties of life. You will no longer care about anything but pleasing Me, and when you know I am pleased, you will be at peace.

Empty yourself into Me: your pride, your desires, your comforts.

> Do not seek honor.
> Do not seek glory.
> Do not seek approval of man.

You are approved by Me. Man's approval is nothing.

> I AM THE ONE WHO ESTABLISHES YOUR WAY BEFORE YOU.
>
> SEEK TO PLEASE ONLY ME.

Don't worry about what man thinks any longer. You don't have time for it. *You have a job to do.* You must do it as I direct, for I *and only I* know what lies ahead.

Leaving Self Behind

Empty yourself into Me. You must die to self to be effective.

I WILL NOT FAIL YOU.

You can trust Me.

You will see the fruit of your labor, so labor well. Be a faithful witness. Be a faithful servant.

You are not to confide in man.

Do not testify of yourself.

Do not seek to please man.

Rather, listen every moment to My Spirit, who will instruct you. Be careful to follow precisely My every command, for only then will the work that I give you proceed as you obey. If you are faithful with the little, I'll give you more.

You will have to rise above all the anxieties that try to plague you. You will have to take flight and soar with My Spirit, leaving self behind. You have spent long enough pleasing self, gratifying your flesh. As you rise above those carnal desires and worries, you must enter into My rest into My shelter.

The Fear of Man

You must stay in sweet communion with Me at all times, pressing into Me as your faithful Father. For as your trust builds, so will your confidence, so will your vision.

For I am preparing one who soars above, who feels comfortable in that realm, who is not pulled here and there by natural anxieties of man. You must go on with Me. This is another step in My plan for you.

I want you to be free from the fear of man.

Only then will you be an effective messenger. Only then will you see the extent to which I have called you.

The fear of man brings a snare.[29]

Fear is tormenting and debilitating.

Faith is liberating and empowering.

Faith frees you from the bondage man tries to put you under.

The devil would have you frozen in fear, unable to heed the Spirit, so it is imperative that you fall onto My grace and press into My faithfulness. For if you rest in My faithfulness, you will be satisfied with no fear.

Rest in My goodness.
Throw yourself onto Me.

I will change your heart. *I will set you free, and you will be free indeed.*[30]

Oh, that you would hearken unto My voice! Then I will make My ways known to you. Then you will see Me at work in you.

The One Who Stands Over His Creation

Rest in My work, for I work even until now as a man tilling a garden. I watch over what I have planted with care. As one who gets up every morning to see the new growth, so am I, eager to see you blossom into that for which I've created you.

No one can say, "He does not care," for I AM the One who stands over His creation, watering and cultivating. You *can* say of Me, "He knows those who are His and gently ushers them into His grace by His tender care."

No more will they say, "Be. Do. Go!" for I am doing a work so quick that they won't have time.

> IF YOU COULD ONLY SEE ALL THAT I HAVE FOR YOU, YOU WOULD NOT GET LOST IN THE MIRE OF THE EVERYDAY CARES AND CONCERNS.

For I seek to introduce you to a better way—free from worry, free from all that burdens down those who have lost their way.

Poised and Ready

Let Me work in you down to every response, every thought, every action. Yes, I do desire for you to be *that* obedient. As one who responds to an emergency call, so you must be when I send you out, giving no concern to what is at hand. For I will work out all that concerns you for your good without you giving it any thought as you respond to My call as you give heed to My promptings.

Seek only My Kingdom. Heed only My voice. Do not heed those voices that would say, "Has He really said thus and so?" for even Eve was carried away with this deception. I told you that you would hear clearly, and it will be so, so don't question that still, small voice inside.

> I WILL TO SPEAK THIS WAY, FOR WHAT MAN IS THERE WHO, WHEN GIVEN A MESSAGE IN HIS EAR, MUST NOT STOP ALL AND LISTEN? FOR I AM NOT ONE TO SHOUT.

I will not constantly shake My children. They must learn to watch expectantly, waiting attentively for My voice. They must yield to Me, for the work that I have to do requires submission from My children. Their time, their will, their concerns, all must bow to My commands, however soft.

Yes, you will hear, but not as man hears, for man seeks only to hear to fulfill a desire. You will hear as one who sits poised and ready, anxious to do as the Master instructs to please only Him.

Elusive Is the Kingdom

Pay attention to My wooings. Give ear to My direction. Don't be so consumed with the everyday routine, for My work is not a man's work. My work is ever-changing, progressing higher and higher.

No man can understand the extent of My workings, yet I choose to reveal to some the inner workings of the Kingdom what eye cannot perceive. You are one who can perceive what My Spirit is doing in the coming days.

Hold fast to that which you've been given. Don't let it slip through your fingers. Elusive is the Kingdom to many. They cannot grasp it. They will not take it as it is. They wish to build their own empires, molding bricks and mortar into edifices for kings, yet the King of kings cannot come in.

They shut him out. They will have none of His ways, none of His workings, none of His children. Even now, He waits to stir them, to test them, to try them in the fire of His Presence in the furnace of affliction—not willingly, though expedient in His plan.

PRECIOUS, PRECIOUS, PRECIOUS TO ME ARE MY SERVANTS WHO WAIT ON ME, GIVING HEED TO MY EVERY COMMAND.

Oh, how I long to instruct them in the Way of Righteousness! Eager of heart are they to do all that I command. Eager of spirit are they to bask in My Presence, waiting on My voice, giving ear to My quiet instruction.

Indistinguishable to the Untrained Eye

Don't be as one who, upon seeing a treasure, backs away in disbelief, who takes a step but won't come any closer. You are to partake of all that I have for you.

Don't be blind to My gracious hand extended toward you. Don't gape at My goodness, yet not enter in. For I have much, much more to lavish upon you, much more waiting on My table.

So, eat, drink, and be full.

Taste of My goodness.

My gracious hand awaits to set you in your place, restoring to you the joy of your salvation, completing in you the good work I have for you. Just wait and see.

> OH, I LONG TO SHOW MYSELF STRONG ON BEHALF OF THOSE WHOSE HEARTS ARE PERFECT TOWARD ME.[31] WHOSE EYES ARE FIXED ON MY COURSE!

Many are they who have forged their own way for naught, but few are they who take My road. For My road is so perfect yet so indistinguishable to the untrained eye. Yielded, yielded are they who find it, yielded to My will, My workings, My ways, yet unbending in their resolution to stand, and after they've done all—to stand.

We're Moving Forward!

Now, even now, My Spirit is calling those who will walk, who will see, who will stand with you on the road laid out plainly for your feet. Don't be dismayed on the journey, for nothing you face, nothing you encounter will be insurmountable. For haven't I said, haven't I faithfully declared that you will walk this road without stumbling? You will be set securely in the place ordained for you. Oh yes, it is so.

> **Keep to the course.**
>> **Keep your eyes open.**
>> **Keep your ears attentive.**
>> **Keep your mouth shut.**
> **Only as I have directed shall you speak.**

Oh, take your stand. Yes, take your position. It's time. No more excuses. We're moving forward! Oh, yes, it's time. Keep your eyes on the course laid out before you. Don't put your eyes on man. Your gaze must be on Me.

Many will fail you. They will stand only as I allow them, but your eyes must not be fixed on them, only on Me. Don't get your eyes focused on man, and you will see clearly as I lead you. Don't pay attention to what man does from day to day. Set your hope only on what I have told you, only on what you have seen in the Spirit, for only My Spirit knows the way, only My Spirit knows the plan.

Out of the Dust

Oh, My child, remember My goodness when you look and do not see with your eyes when you listen and do not hear with your ears.

It is then when you must stand on who I AM.

You will not always see what is encouraging to the naked eye. You will not always hear what you want to, but as you remember My Love, you will not be disheartened. On the contrary, when you encounter disappointment, just realize that I am bringing your will into subjection to Me, which is not always easy.

As you look to what is unseen, your spirit will begin to arise out of the dust and *mount up with wings as eagles*.[32]

Only when your hope is in Me and Me alone will you soar, and soar you will!

Eyes Wide Open

Watch. Wait.

Learn.

Don't size up a situation upon first glance. Don't set your sights on the natural. Don't listen, as others do, with just their natural ears.

Wait for My voice.

Don't look with your eyes but with Mine. Yes, don't speak your words—only Mine—then you will begin to see all the things I've said would come to pass. Yes, you will look with My eyes and see so many things others can't. You will see their hurts and scars, their fears and worries, their needs, and even their wants. You will know and won't have to guess. You will see and won't have to wonder. You will hear and won't be deaf to their cry.

Yes, all will seem so clear as you wait on Me as you lean upon My Spirit. You will see things by the Spirit not perceptible in the natural. You will see with the eye of the Spirit, so watch expectantly. Wait in anticipation for dreams and visions. They will come.

There's a reason you do what you do. There's a reason you see the things you see. It's not an accident. It didn't just happen. No, I have a purpose. I know what I am doing. You must learn. Look with your spiritual eyes, and you'll see. Open up your ears to hear. Don't be deaf.

Don't hold back. Let that river flow.

Don't be hesitant.

It's time.

In a Place Called Blessed

Will you not learn? Have I not told you time and again that all My words will not fall to the ground? Nothing I have said in your ear will fail to come to pass, and yet you have not believed Me, the Author of life. I will establish you among men. I will set you in your place securely.

Nothing established has been established in futility, for My Word goes out to perform the good thing that I purpose. My purpose is to set you in a place that others call blessed, for My blessing will be upon you as you follow in the way as you walk before Me in obedience.

> Don't turn to the side.
>
> Don't set yourself before men.
>
> I will do that.

I will cause those who are called to hear to make a way for you to speak. You will not have to do a thing. There will be no effort expended on your part to make the road smooth, no effort necessary to be heard.

Just listen to My voice and do only as instructed, for I am calling you to be a voice to the many along the way.

Filtering Out the Noise

Learn to walk precisely on the path set out for you. Don't let others persuade you along another.

> Only by heeding My voice at every step
> > will you perceive the right path.
>
> Only by filtering out the noise
> > will you be able to discern
> > > what My Spirit would have you do.

For yours is a path less traveled. For only the few dare take this way. Not by anything you have done, nor will do, are you going to walk this journey.

My Spirit will take you along the path.

Do not fear.
> Just rest.

For My working is complete, lacking nothing. Don't listen to those who would try to pervert the good that I am doing. Their eyes cannot see, their ears cannot hear, but you hear, so don't be concerned with other voices.

Be satisfied with the manna I give you, for I sustain all things, even your way.

> Rest in Me securely.
>
> Take no thought for tomorrow.

Busy, Busy, Busy

Even a child walking on the way knows to follow Daddy. Even a horse knows and understands commands from his master, yet My people are devoid of knowledge, knowing not the right way, perceiving nothing.

> Oh, I would that they would heed My calling, listening carefully to My voice!

They fill their lives with nothing that will satisfy. They look for Me, yet don't find Me in their many activities. I long to make a way for them to walk satisfied in My Presence, yet they will have none of it.

> Busy, busy, busy are My people, but not busy about My business, not concerned with My workings—only their own.

Nothing Reserved

Your time is My concern. Your business is My concern. Your every action is My concern. I want to perfect you in such a way that it will cause you to yield every part of your life to Me.

I WANT ALL OF YOU, NOTHING RESERVED.

It's not enough to wait on Me once a day. It's not enough to listen to Me occasionally throughout your day.

I WANT ALL OF YOU, ALL THE TIME.

I want your every response to be directed by Me.

Rid yourself of useless chatter.

Rid yourself of useless worry, concern over anything.

For *I will perfect that which concerns you*[33] to the -nth degree. Give no thought to how or what I'm going to do down the road. I want you to listen at every step, taking care to wait for direction. I'll show you how to deal with the kids if you will wait on Me.

Like an intricate pattern, I'm weaving your life into that which pleases Me, so don't be concerned with your life, only My workings, for My workings encompass your very life.

Take hold of My Spirit as you begin to fly. Grab on and don't let go, for I will not drop you.

WALK WITH ME.

They Have Left

Everything *you* see, everything *you* hear can be seen and heard in the natural. Everything *I* see and everything *I* hear cannot. You must see with My eyes and hear with My ears.

> YOU MUST TOSS AWAY YOUR OLD GARMENT AND BE CLOTHED WITH MY RAIMENT.[34]

Many will say, "Come up here. Go down there," yet I will say, "Be still!" Many who are tossed back and forth like the wind will gather around hoping, yet they have come to the wrong place.

> I AM HE WHO CARRIES THEM, FEEDS THEM, NOURISHES THEM TO HEALTH, YET THEY WILL RUN AFTER MAN.

Nobody, nobody, nobody can say that I do not feed My sheep, yet My sheep have left. They have run off only to find they are lost and alone, longing to come back. Each and every one must be found and brought back.

> I WILL HAVE IT NO OTHER WAY.

Only Tasted, Barely Touched

The time has come for your eyes to be opened to the realities of My Kingdom. You may think that you have seen, but you haven't, for My Kingdom extends far beyond and above what you have seen thus far.

You have only tasted, barely touched the fringe of all that I have for you.

> Enter in by My grace.
> Enter in by My mercy.

For man gets nothing from Me by any other means.

> All that you are today and all that you will be tomorrow is wrapped up in who I AM, so seek Me continually. Give yourself wholly over to My grace.

Even the animals know My hand in their affairs, yet My people cannot see Me work. They do not give Me credit. They will not attribute to Me the work that I do in their lives.

> See Me in everything.
> See My hand in your affairs—in every detail.
> I AM there.
> Know Me.

Shared by Laura Wilcott

Upward, Higher, Closer

Fret not. Just listen to My instruction, for I will tell you what to do and instruct you in the way.

I DO NOT SPEAK IN RIDDLES TO THOSE IN THE KINGDOM.

I do not wish to hide My Face, yet at times I must. I want to cleanse the heart and make it strong.

HARDSHIP IS A KEY INGREDIENT IN MY PLAN.

Now, you must alter your course at My command. You must forsake the way you've trodden and take the path that leads upward, higher, closer, leading into My very Presence. I will change you as you press into Me. Don't be anxious as to how or when.

DELIGHT IN ME.

LET ME BE YOUR RESTING PLACE.

Oh, what I have for you, you can only imagine! What I have for you, you can only dream! There is no question that I seek good for you, but with it, there will be hardship.

Don't be anxious, little one, for I have you in My hands. I will perform that good work in you. I will see it through to completion.

OH, JUST REST IN MY FINISHED WORK.[35]

NEEDLESSLY DO YOU STRIVE TO BE, FOR I AM.[36]

Bought with a Price

Step out of the way. Don't keep My work from progressing.

Be free from what man thinks.

Cut off any ties to the opinions of others. You need only say what I say and do what I do—nothing more, nothing less. Keep your eyes on Me and your heart on what *I* think.

You don't have to prove anything to anybody. I will testify of you.

Don't be a man-pleaser.

Don't be concerned with what people think.

Be concerned with what *I* think and

what *I* say!

Don't be caught up with the affairs of life. Don't be distracted by what distracts the world.

YOU ARE NOT YOUR OWN. *YOU ARE BOUGHT WITH A PRICE.*[37]

You must wait for instructions.

In the Hull of the Boat

Oh, let Me be the One who calms the storm! At My command, the waves subside, the winds cease, the sea is stilled.

Yes, you may think that life is a storm that can't be calmed, but the storm isn't out there. It's inside.

> FOR WHEN YOU ENTER INTO THAT PEACEFUL PLACE I HAVE FOR YOU, WHEN YOU STEP INTO THAT SECRET PLACE UNDER THE SHADOW OF MY WINGS,[38] THEN YOU WILL SEE, THEN YOU WILL UNDERSTAND THERE WAS NO STORM AT ALL.

Why do you think I slept in the hull of that boat? They accused Me, too, of not caring.[39]

> YES, THEY ACCUSED THE ONE THAT CARRIED THEM OF OLD,[40] THAT WAS SLAIN FROM THE FOUNDATION FOR THEM![41]

They couldn't see the storm raging inside them. They wanted Me to calm what they could see, what they could hear, but I desire to bring you to a better place, a place of rest, far from what your eyes see and your ears hear, in the hull of the boat—asleep, at rest, secure.

Emptied Out, Only to Be Filled

Ambitions—they rob one of the need to wait. *But they that wait upon the Lord shall renew their strength; they shall mount up with wings as eagles. They shall run, and not be weary; and they shall walk, and not faint.*[42]

Those who are led by My Spirit learn to wait on Me. They have no ambitions. They wait on Me to empty out their will to Mine. They wait on Me to accomplish the work there is to do.

THEY REST IN MY FINISHED WORK.

They do not aspire, only retire.

They have no resolutions.

They wait on My Spirit to perform in them the needed adjustments. Let go of the things that hold you back. Your pride stands in My way.

ALL THAT YOU ARE TO EVER BE IS ROLLED UP IN WHAT I DESIRE TO MAKE OF YOU.

My plans are to fashion you, mold you, make you into *a vessel prepared for every good work.*[43]

INTO MY FIRE

Open your heart to receive the necessary adjustments to your will. Fly open wide the doors to change, for I have much change in store for you in the coming days. You may think that much change has taken place, but compared to what I have for you, it has only been a fraction.

> FOR I DESIRE YOUR WHOLE BEING,
> YOUR INNER SOUL.

You can't see, as of yet, the full extent of the change to take place. It will come like a strong wind blowing away everything that is not nailed down by My Spirit. It will be like a purifying fire. No flesh can stand in its presence. No will can remain unbendable when it sweeps over.

> SNAP GO THE EMBERS! MY SMOLDERING FIRE CONSUMES THE WILL AND LEAVES NOTHING THAT INHIBITS.

Throw yourself into My fire. Cast away the doubt you have of My goodness.

All that you are is in My hands. You are secure, in a secure place.

> BE ENVELOPED IN MY LOVE.
> BE WASHED OVER WITH PURE WATER.

Shared by Laura Wilcott

I Work Alone!

I know what you are made of.

I fashioned you.

I knit you by hand.

I know that you cannot bear much weight. It's My desire to accomplish that which I have begun in you, to build the house in the manner prescribed by My Father. This house can only stand at My command. Oh, many think they are the builders, that they are the craftsmen, yet they are blind to the truth.

I AM the Master Craftsman. I work alone!

I fashion My house as I see fit, not as man directs. I have given them a spirit of stupor, so they are deceived. They believe theirs is the glory. They see themselves as instruments of My Spirit, and yet they follow their own paths, looking to their own wisdom for direction.

Many are just like this, just as deceived, just as empty, just as shallow of spirit. They follow them, not knowing where they go, not seeing the futility of their efforts. I am doing a work even now, a work to guide them from their foolishness to walk in My ways. There are some who will hear and turn from their foolishness. These are the first fruits. They have already begun to come in. The others will have to walk a harder road.

No Better Time

There's no better time to be yielded to My workings as the present, for My work must be accomplished in complete harmony with the work of the Father. As He does it, I do it too.

> EMPTY YOURSELF,
>
> MOMENT BY MOMENT,
>
> INTO MY GRACE.

I will sustain you through every trial. Don't look at the difficulties.

> JUST FALL ONTO MY GRACE
>
> TIME AND AGAIN.

I will carry you, so be encouraged, for the Lord God is on your side, ever working for your good. If you could only see all the good I have for you.

> Don't be downcast. Rise above!
>
> Walk with your head up!
>
> YOU WILL REIGN!

Starving

I have set a table before you.

> Come and eat to your delight!
>
> Come and partake of all I have set before you!

Many starve because they refuse to sit at My table. They will not acknowledge My bounty. They choose their delusions. They are satisfied with lack. Their self-righteous, self-imposed religion keeps them in bondage to *the elementary principles of the world*.[44]

They will not accept freedom. They sit at a table set by man. It is empty. They go hungry. They wonder why they are not satisfied. They thirst for more, yet their thirst goes unsatisfied, for they refuse to get up and leave man's table to sup at Mine. They stay at their place starving.

The host is pleased while the children go hungry, while the guests famish. His table is full of guests, yet he has nothing to give them. My table is overflowing with choice morsels: meat and wine and every kind of Life-giving food.

> Who will come and eat?
>
> Who will partake of My bounty?

My table awaits. The places are set.

Can you say that anything is too hard for Me? Can you think of anything that I cannot do? Can you understand any of My works?

Seekers of My Kingdom

Never before has My Glory been so available! I am ready to shower on the many a Spirit of Glory. Their hope will no longer be in what they see but only in Me.

> Shout! Rejoice! For My Glory has gone out even now. It has been shed abroad to those seekers of My Kingdom who seek Me night and day.

You seekers, you faithful servants of the Lord, stand and walk in the Glory of My Presence, for it will be round about you! Your eyes will be light, your steps brightened before you. You will no longer grope along the way.

> My Light has come.

You will see it. You will bask in its warmth. You will not fear the dark places any longer, *for they will be illuminated.*

> Light, My Light, is on the horizon! As the day dawns and the Morning Star rises in your hearts, rejoice, for His Glory has risen upon you.[45] His Light has consumed you!

Your Very Great Reward

My words are for this hour. You must see in the Spirit, or you will not be ready. Put down every thought that is opposed to those things I am saying.

Take up your faith, for every path among men is laid out plainly for those who will hear and obey. They need not set about to make their way. I direct every step regardless of their plans, regardless of their strivings to attain their way.

Only in Me can you perceive the way. Only in My direction can you ascertain the true and certain path to follow.

> **Don't be timid along the way.**
> **Don't stand back. March forward!**
> **I AM your confidence—*your very great reward*.**[46]
> **I will equip you for the journey.**
> **I will see you through.**
> **You are not alone.**

I am by your side, so stand, walk, and see what I have for you. All your troubles will seem as nothing. All your worries will disappear, for I cause you to rise above them to ride on the high places.

Now is the time for you to hear what the Spirit is saying. Do not close your ear to My voice. You will hear more. You will perceive more. You must be attentive. Do not be distracted. Do not look around at your surroundings. They are temporal.

My Kingdom is eternal.

Shared by Laura Wilcott

Run from It!

No matter what's going on around you, you must enter in. Don't hold back, for neither man nor spirit can see the full result of what I ask you to do at any moment.

> Only *My* Spirit knows the benefits and rewards of your obedience.
>
> Only *My* Spirit sees through the course of events to the manifestation of My Glory, so don't be afraid of man.

Don't look to man for honor, acknowledgment, or esteem. Don't give any thought to man's approval—run from it!

> **Run from honor,**
>
> **man's glory,**
>
> **praise.**

Don't seek it out, for it will not bring about My Glory.

A Higher Dimension

Open up as I enable you to flow continually with the wind of My Spirit. It can be any moment of any day in spite of your circumstances. Man is limited by circumstances—not Me!

> I HAVE PLACED YOU AS I WISH FOR MY DELIGHT, SO DON'T BE TIMID TO TAKE YOUR PLACE.

As the wind blows, you can see the effects, but you can't see the wind. As the wind of My Spirit blows on your life, don't resist.

> OPEN UP TO MY WORKINGS.
>
> OPEN UP TO MY PROMPTINGS.

Be not as those who honor Me as others watch yet deny Me in the dark. Be not double-minded, swayed by circumstances and surroundings.

Fasten your garments around you.

> **Get ready to run.**
>
> **Prepare for action.**

For I am taking you into a higher realm—one of testings and trials, one of fire and burnings. It will not be as you suppose. Your Creator stands ready to carry you into this higher dimension, so stand and watch and wait. It will be as I say.

Shared by Laura Wilcott

What Tender Care, What Loving Kindness!

The realm I have for you is one of action, not contemplation. Many wish to sit and be ministered to, yet I *will* to minister *through*. My counsel in these days will stand. They are designed to build you up and strengthen you. They are for the express purpose of setting you in your place.

Don't take the counsel of the Lord lightly. Give it due attention and respect. Don't overlook My instructions, even though they are many. For My instruction is vital for your growth. I wish for you to see My workings as they come to pass in your life. Every day, you will see My plans unfold before you. Every day, you will hear what My Spirit desires. Gently will I mold you. Gently will My hands fashion you into a vessel for My glory. You will know My gentle touch.

> What tender care I use to fashion My vessels! What loving-kindness I show them day by day! If they could only see My loving hand upon them, if they could only hear My whispers of mercy in their ear, they would run to Me; they would rush to My feet.

Yet My people, calloused and slow to hear, miss My wooings. They seek activity and man's approval. They crave attention but not from Me.

My Finished Work

See to it that you give due attention to what I say. Don't regard man or esteem him too highly, for all that is in man, *the lust of the flesh, the lust of the eyes, and the pride of life*[47] must be burned off. I see the dross. I see the imperfections.

I *will* perfect My people.

Keep your eyes on Me, not My servants. I *will* to burn away that which clouds My Glory.

Remain in Me. Stay in My fire.

Rest in My work.

You are right. It is My work.

Rest in My finished work.

My Desire

You must see that never will I ask of you more than what I have already birthed in your spirit, what I have already deposited inside of you.

> LET EACH DAY BURST FORTH AS ONE THAT I HAVE ORDAINED, WALKING UPRIGHTLY AND VICTORIOUSLY IN ALL THAT HAS BEEN ESTABLISHED FOR YOU TO WALK.

See each moment as one preordained for you to rise above your circumstances and shine as a light shines. I will you to be a peacemaker.

LISTEN TO ME.

Don't forget to lean on Me when dealing with the children. Don't forget My counsel.

My desire is to see you walk in My direction each and every moment, not giving heed to your own thoughts and plans, emptying yourself into My will, not taking over the reins, not operating out of your own wisdom.

As you submit to Me, you will reap the rewards of obedience. As you empty yourself out into Me, you will walk in more revelation. I require death to all that is in you. Only then will you truly be free to walk in My Life. Only then will that seed take root and grow.

Seek only Me. In all your seeking, seek Me. Don't be blown to the side by those seeking glory. Just don't pay them any attention. That is what they seek.

Molded for This Hour

No one knows the Father except the Son and those to whom He chooses to reveal Him.[48] I have chosen to reveal Him to you.

> WILL YOU NOT LEARN? I HAVE MOLDED YOU FOR THIS HOUR, AND YET YOU SAY, "HAVE YOU REALLY?" I HAVE SET YOU IN YOUR PLACE, AND YOU SAY, "WHY?"

Stop questioning My choice!

Stop questioning and go on!

It is not your place to question what I am doing. It is not your place to question My election. You must respond to My workings. You must carry the mantle I have given you and be what I have ordained you to be—with no reservations. No time, no more time should be given to questioning!

MOVE ON!

MOVE ON BY MY GRACE!

MOVE ON IN THE SPIRIT TO HIGHER HEIGHTS, INTO GREATER GLORY.

Move Over

It is not about you! Do not think that any longer. Do not entertain any thoughts about you.

> THIS IS ABOUT ME AND MY WORKINGS,
> ME AND MY ABILITIES, ME AND MY PLANS.
> ABSOLUTELY NOTHING HINGES ON YOU![49]

You are not at the center of anything! I am *building up a house*,[50] one that is not as you have known. This new vessel is empty of self. You must be empty—empty of all your aspirations, desires, dreams, plans, cares, worries, concerns, hopes, ego, pride, ambitions—everything that will stand in My way. That is why you must get out of the way!

> Move over. Get out of *My* way.

I will lead you with no effort of your own. Empty yourself into Me. Don't act like you had anything to do with My excellent plans, my wondrous works.

> **Just magnify Me.**
> GLORIFY ME.

Point them to Me. They know it was Me anyway. *Don't stand in the way, trying to enjoy the moment.*

> I AM the moment.
> ENJOY ME!

Beyond Their Eyes, Into My Realm

You see things as man sees them, but there is a day coming when you will look and not see what others see. You will not see things only in the natural. You will see beyond their eyes—into My realm. You will see everything as it truly is.

Speak only what you hear Me speaking. Do only what you see Me doing then you will not speak out of turn.

FOR THOSE WHO SPEAK ONLY WHAT THEY HEAR ME SPEAKING HAVE A CONFIDENCE AND AN AUTHORITY THAT OTHERS WILL RECOGNIZE THAT OTHERS WILL ACKNOWLEDGE.

Only what you hear, only what you see with your eyes, only what's placed before you, makes a difference in the Kingdom.

Your eye sees nothing of real value.

It can only see what's temporal.

Stop looking with your natural eyes.

Stop listening with your natural ears.

Stop thinking in natural terms.

YOU ARE SPIRITUAL.

Shared by Laura Wilcott

My Kingdom is spiritual.

I AM Spirit.

The natural mind has very little to do with anything of any real importance.

Throw off your old thinking. Be renewed in your mind. Be renewed to what My Spirit has been telling you.

You are what I say you are!

You will do what I say you will do!

Only to Be Carried

It is not necessary that you grasp the reality of everything I have said right now, for I am making it real to you. My timing is perfect. It will stand.

You have only to be carried.

I'll carry you into what I have for you. Don't be anxious when you see new things approaching. Don't be intimidated because your spirit has been created for this realm.

Your flesh must die. It cannot enter into My realm. I will do this work. I will see it through to completion. I will make it happen, so rest, rest, rest!

A sail exerts no effort. It just opens up. A soaring bird exerts no effort. A floating leaf in a river exerts no effort.

Oh, little do you know of My unfathomable grace! Little do you see, thus far, of My far-reaching plan!

The Vastness, the Immensity

Only in Me can you fully see what lies ahead.

Only in Me can you be.

Nothing, absolutely nothing, stands in your way. Nothing can hinder you from tasting of the sweet manna I have for you.

You may think the calling I have placed on your life is irrevocable, and yes, it is. I have made you, called you, ordained you to walk as a light, to heed the instructions given to you at each and every moment.

Get ready, for My plan that is in effect right now involves major changes in your overall outlook on life.

> NO ONE CAN FORESEE THE VASTNESS, EVEN THE IMMENSITY OF WHAT I HOLD IN STORE FOR YOU. FOR MY THOUGHTS I THINK TOWARD YOU ARE THOUGHTS OF PEACE.[51]

So Much Better

Do not say in your heart, "Give me peace," for it has been given as a flood that breaks the dam.

> **MY PEACE, MY SWEET PRESENCE IS ALL ABOUT YOU, WAITING TO CARRY YOU UP HIGHER.**

Don't resist My counsel in the coming days, but yield, yield to Me and see all that I have spoken over you fulfilled. Yes, rest. For in your resting is victory. In your resting is strength for the journey ahead.

Be at peace, for I will carry you to My desired destination. I will make a way where there seems to be no way. A door stands open before you.

[*How do I enter in?*]
WE'LL WALK TOGETHER.
WE'LL STAND AND ENTER IN AS ONE,
SO DON'T BE AFRAID.

Don't be hesitant. Don't stand back, but press on through, for what awaits you on the other side is so much better than you can imagine. Have an attitude of readiness.

BE AT PEACE.
REST.

Trivial Pursuits

No more time needs to be given to concern over yourself. You've spent enough time consumed with what you want to think about, what you want to dwell on. What about what I want? Does what I think count? Shouldn't My thoughts be ever on your mind, not your trivial pursuits?

How will you be full for the task if your mind stays on what doesn't satisfy? How will you be ready when I say "Go!" if you're daydreaming? Keep your mind on Me. Let Me be your focus!

> LET ME BE YOUR PRAISE, YOUR HONOR, YOUR GLORY! I AM WORTHY OF IT ALL.

I am the only thing that matters. What you focus on won't satisfy any need. It won't heal any heartache or mend any relationship. It won't comfort the torn or heal an open wound. No, only My Life flowing through you has power.

You can't do anything, so why so much emphasis on self? It's *a hindrance, a weight,* baggage. Throw it off. *Take up your cross and follow Me.*[52] You'll have no regrets. It's so much better My way.

> IT'S SO MUCH SWEETER WITH ME AS YOUR LOVE, YOUR OBJECT OF AFFECTION.

Don't be enamored with what enamors the world. You are not of the world. Be separate.

They Come Close with Their Lips

Generations and generations call on Me and yet do not fully see My Kingdom realm. They search for Me, looking to man, seeking out man, honoring man, yet I know man is nothing. Man can do nothing, say nothing, or be nothing apart from My workings.

They honor what is not honorable. They give no thought to their ways. I long to carry them. They will have none of Me. *They come close to Me with their mouths and honor me with their lips, but their hearts are far from Me.*[53]

> Know your Master's voice.
>
> Hear Him in your ear.

Listen carefully.

Watch expectantly.

> Be at peace.

Know the time is right for you to step into the waters of My river, for you to sail by My winds. Each and every day, I draw you closer to the realities of My Kingdom. Each and every day, I draw you higher into Me into the Secret Place, into that place of rest.

> Enter in!

He Will Be Evicted

Little One, don't be troubled, for that comes from the enemy. Don't be condemned, for that is a work of Satan.

> Run to Me, and I'll carry your burden.
> Hide in Me, and I'll shelter you.
> Throw yourself onto Me,
> and I'll keep you safe from the enemy.

> **Recognize his workings.**
>
> **Know his schemes.**

Don't be ignorant of his devices.[54] Remember, *he prowls around you, waiting for an opportunity.*[55]

Resist him firmly. He does not have a place in what I'm doing in you.

> **He will be evicted.**
>
> **Stand.**

Many Enlisted

No man has the answers to your questions but Me. No one can say anything to you that clears the way as My Spirit can. I have enlisted many to speak by My Spirit. I have enlisted you to do the same.

Don't let man be the light I am to be. For I have said to follow My Light. I will make your path lit before you. I will lead you in the way. I'll guide you.

Depend on Me.

Don't look to man. Don't be afraid of man.

Speak what I have you speak!

Listen to Me always. Next time, listen and speak My words. Do not let the fear of man dominate you.

Speak up!

Listen in your ear. I'll instruct you how to answer.

Be at peace.

Don't be troubled. All that I have said to you concerning your life and things to come has come to you through the direction of My Spirit. Don't take the things I give you lightly. Be at peace. For as I have said, I am making the way before you, so be at peace. In a little while, all will seem as a dream!

Jump into This River!

Coming to Me need not be an effort. Don't be concerned with how and what you're going to say. Just rest. Wait.

Let Me speak to your heart.

You can respond to Me. You can follow Me. I'll lead you into communion. I'll lead you into that place I would have you be. So wait.

Be at peace.

Step into this higher place I have for you. Jump into this river! Love will carry you to this place.

Don't hold back.

Discern My voice.

Listen attentively.

I will speak to you along the way. I will confide in you with each step you take.

Don't fail to listen.

Don't fail to heed My voice.

Don't get caught up in your daily affairs. Stay alert to My instructions. That communion you long for, that fellowship you desire, is available as you talk to Me through everything as you throw yourself onto Me at each turn.

Shared by Laura Wilcott

Drink Deeply

I have so many things to tell you, so many things to teach you, but you aren't ready.

> I LONG FOR YOU TO GROW UP, TO STOP REACTING IN THE FLESH, TO BE CONTROLLED BY MY SPIRIT, TO BE SUSTAINED BY MY LOVE.

My Love conquers all, all your fears, all your anxieties. Everything responds to My Love except the flesh. You are a vessel that must be full of My Love—complete, lacking nothing.

REST IN ME.

Continue to rest, not looking to yourself to complete anything, for I will be glorified in My workings. Your longings will not go unsatisfied. Yes, you will drink and eat and be filled. You won't go away thirsty, for I will quench your thirst with My very Presence.

DRINK DEEPLY OF MY LOVE.

Have Another Helping!

Come. I bid you.

Come! Drink! Taste of that sweet wine offered to you. Eat! Be full! Don't go hungry. I want you to be filled, satisfied, overflowing. Don't stay away from My table.

I'm waiting for you.

Take what I've given you as a precious treasure and hold it close.

Don't bury it in the sand.

Don't give it out at will.

Don't let it wash away with the tide.

No, hold it close. For in the words that I give you, in the very breath that I breathe into your life, is Life—abundant, free, full, and overflowing.

Take it as a choice morsel. Consume it. Don't stare in wonder, then walk away unsatisfied. Partake! Dig in! *Have another helping!*

Don't be shy. There's plenty! You weren't asked to the table to go away hungry. You were expressly invited to My meal to fill up what is lacking to satisfy your need.

Strategically Placed

Established are you to do My will, yet not willing. Strategically placed for My purposes are you, laid in and among fine gold, fitted securely. Now is the time to see your place, to rest in who you are created to be.

Don't look at the circumstances or the surroundings. Don't look at the people or the situation.

Be willing. Be open to My leading.

Walk where it is plain. Don't force anything. I will make it plain, each step. Your willingness is essential. Take care not to establish your own way or forge your own path.

My Spirit will lead.

You will know for certain. You will easily discern the path to follow, or you will not enter in. I do not desire for you to wander in the dark. No, I will not have it. Your path will be lit before you, so do not move unless you see the way. Do not step into the dark.

I am able to make it clear to you. I am able to make you certain.

Step in My steps.
Wait on Me.

Learn to not forge ahead. Learn to wait on direction and instruction. This is very important.

[*How do I speak?*] I will open a door for you.

All your efforts and struggles to be can only be realized through My work, not yours; through My will, not yours; through My plans and purposes, not yours.

As the Clouds Full of Rain

Make certain you know the way before you take a step.

BE STILL AND KNOW MY WAY.

Give thought to My words. Impress them on your heart. Be at peace in My Presence. Call on My Name and give Me praise. Rejoice before Me. Then you will rise as the clouds full of rain. You will fill up in My Presence. Then you will rain on those I've placed around you. You will do nothing but shower on them the Love of My Spirit.

Take no thought to your plans of action. I have a course set for you.

JUST BE STILL AND KNOW MY PRESENCE.

Wait and see if I don't cause you to be a light by My very Presence. Don't be concerned with how. Don't make plans; only listen every moment.

Take what I've given you for My glory. Trust Me to accomplish in you the work I *will* to work in you.

LET THAT LOVE FLOW NATURALLY FROM MY SPIRIT OUT TO THE MANY.

Don't set out ahead of Me. Don't be as one who asks directions and then goes another way before the light has turned green. Be willing to wait on Me. Only My perfect timing will bring results. "Only by My Spirit," says the Lord.

Those Precious Few

Oh, if you only knew My thoughts toward you! The time is coming when men's heart will fail. They will rise up and be dashed to pieces. They will reap a harvest they do not want. They will be struck to the heart with grief and anguish, torn in two by despair.

Oh, but you will rise up. You will not falter, for you will see My salvation. You will see My Glory dawning as the morning sun. You will rejoice in that day, for it will be light around you as the noonday sun.

Keep your eyes fixed on My Word, on My goodness, on My tender care. Don't be swayed by what you see and hear, by what goes on around you.

Oh, My Kingdom awaits those precious few who cast everything onto Me and behold My Glory!

You have never seen such as this—a people wholly surrendered in My Presence. Yet you will see it, for I am calling them even now. They will hate their lives even to death. They will want nothing but to please Me. You are one.

You will stand.

You will walk.

You will see.

Shared by Laura Wilcott

Seize the Moment!

Every time you venture out without Me, you cause damage.

[I didn't ask for the Lord's direction and made a mess.]

You can expect similar results every time you step out without Me. Don't be surprised at the mess you make when you try to take things into your own hands, then you expect Me to mop up after you.

Your dependence on Me needs to be moment by moment. I long to teach you how to press into Me.

> **Don't be stubborn.**
> **Don't be willfully disobedient as I call out to you.**
> Lean on Me every moment.

Don't make your own path. Seize the moment to be wholly directed in your responses. Don't miss My ever-present help in times of trouble.

Your Ever-Present Help

Don't think you know better. Listen before you act. Listen before you decide a course of action. For I will instruct you in everything. I will lead you gently over the briers and thorns through the rough places. Next time, as you're contemplating which way to go, turn to My Spirit inside and say, "Help."

>FOR I AM YOUR EVER-PRESENT HELP
>
>IN TIMES OF TROUBLE.[56]

Don't look to man. Wait on Me. I know waiting is not easy, but it's worthwhile. Just trust Me. I'll work things out. Don't pave a way.

>I CAN BE TRUSTED.

Oh, yes, you've seen your error. Yes, you've judged correctly. Now is the time to yield. Now is the time to lay down your pride, your agendas, your will and follow Me.

To Be Deposited

Prepared are you for the task I have set down for you. You need to relinquish your efforts to control even the slightest detail of My plan, for you are never to try to orchestrate My workings, for they are beyond your comprehension.

Let go of your plans for your loved ones. Mine are so much better!

Just wait. You'll see.

All that I have for you, all that I hold in My hands will be deposited as I have said.

You need not wonder how and when. For as you open up more and more, you will begin to fill up in My Presence, bask in My warmth, be caressed with My gentle touch, and see that what I have for you, what I hold in My hands, is so much better, so much broader, so much deeper than you can imagine than you can ever dream.

So wake up. Awake to My realities.

Yes, the possibilities are limitless.
Just believe.

Oh, My child, you're limiting yourself. I have no limits.

Where Will It End?

Don't be overwhelmed with the day or what it brings. For as you launch out in My Spirit, as you spread your wings, you will see how easily I can manage your day, how easily I can bring everything into order.

Will you trust Me?

Will you give Me every detail? Will you hold My hand as I usher you through the door that stands open before you?

Can I be trusted?

Can you dare to give Me your stack of responsibilities and allow Me to sort through it, choosing what I deem necessary? Can you dare to let Me make your to-do list?

Can you let go?

Am I faithful?

Will you give up your pen, your phone, your calendar to Me and allow Me to say when, where, and how? What about your friends? "Where will it end?" you might say. And I would say, "Until I have all of you with nothing reserved."

Holding On, Missing Out

My children are so distracted, pulled here and there by others, enticements that appeal to their flesh. It is so much easier to please others when self is on the throne.

What is at stake: your pride, your name, your position, your standing? Isn't My approval what matters? How can you call Me Lord when you insist on managing things?

My people are like children holding on to a piece of candy with white knuckles, teeth clenched, refusing to let go when, all the while, their daddy owns the candy store and longs to give them so much more but can't.

They rush in before Daddy to find a few old pieces on the floor and steal away behind the counter, hoping Daddy won't see, when all the while, He longed to walk in together and boost His child up and fill his bag to the brim, and yet the child will not listen.

He stubbornly hangs onto his prize, not heeding his daddy's voice, not listening for his call. He says, "Daddy won't see."

Oh, when will My children learn?

WHEN WILL THEY UNDERSTAND MY GOODNESS?

WHEN WILL THEY SEE MY GRACE?

You have seen many things and heard wonders, yet only in the Secret Place will you find rest.

Get Your Running Shoes On

Yes, what I've spoken in your ear will surely come to pass. Precious child, wait in expectation for My work to be fulfilled.

Yes, be expectant. Be ready.

Oh, it will be as I have said! It will be glorious!
Get your running shoes on. Stretch your muscles.

Get on your mark! Get set!

For it will be as a runner running in a race. You won't look back.

You won't dawdle.

You won't stumble.

No, you will set your sights on the goal.

You will be off!

It may seem, right now, that you've been running in slow motion, but not for long! For I have you as a runner in My race. This race will be like none you have or could ever imagine. For My plan is to carry you swiftly into all I have for you, all I have prepared for you.

In God's Pickup Truck

My child, look at what I've done so far. Look at how you've traveled. *I've* propelled you. *I've* carried you. You know you didn't have anything to do with it. You've just been along for the ride.

What makes you think anything will change? Just sit back and hold on. I'm in the driver's seat. I'm in control of the wheel.

[*I was thinking about how many people think they are in control of their lives when I saw a pickup truck in my mind's eye with God at the wheel. There was a toy car in the bed of the truck with someone at the steering wheel.*]

Yes, My child, I let My children play car for a while because that's what they want to do, yet all the while, I'm the One who is really at the wheel. They just don't know it yet.

They honk their horn and use their signals. They push the brakes when they've had enough, and they use the gas when they want to go, yet they don't understand why they keep going where they didn't want to go and end up where they did not plan to be.

Finally, after they have had quite enough and get out of their little car, they realize they've been in Mine all along.

[*I could see someone crawling out of the toy car and tapping on the window of God's pickup. He motions for them to come up and join Him—in the passenger seat, of course!*]

Shared by Laura Wilcott

Close Beside You

What happened to your resolve to do anything for Me? Why so hesitant?

[*I started seeing what You might ask of me.*]

AM I NOT FAITHFUL?

Haven't I proven time and again My goodness, My grace, My mercy?
Walk on this path set out for you.

Yes, it's *My* path.

[*Lord, it's a little scary.*]

That's because you are thinking carnally. *Perfect love casts out fear.*[57]

Remember My grace that has been poured out for you so many times. Remember *My mercies that are new every morning.*[58] Remember *My Love shed abroad in your heart.*[59] Take heart. Be encouraged, for *I will never leave you nor forsake you.*[60]

I stand close beside you in the night. I watch over your way.

OH, KNOW MY PEACE.

FEEL MY TOUCH.

SEE MY HAND.

Praise Stills the Avenger

Anxious and worried are you, but you needn't be, for I am well able to cause everything I have said to come to pass. You do not need to struggle or to strive anymore, for I will perform it without your concern, without your effort. Just rest in Me, delight in Me, and trust Me to work it all out as I have said. Don't be concerned with times. For My timing is perfect.

Be at peace.

You see what steals your peace. Walk another way. Don't take that path. No, I have not set it before you. You must turn away when you see yourself going down another way apart from My Spirit.

Choose Life.[61]

Remember, *praise stills the avenger.*[62] Praise arrests, even destroys, what the enemy seeks to do.

Be captivated by My Love.
Praise will carry you there.
Enter in.

There Is No Other

In the multitude of offerings man has to offer, among all the sacrifices man tries to make, within all the promises man hopes to fulfill, where am I?

Man has nothing to give Me that I don't already possess. Man adds nothing to My work. No, man is altogether sinful, blind, and deaf. He is full of greed, envy, and strife. No, I don't want what man wants to give.

I AM—THERE IS NO OTHER.[63]

Oh, that man would see Me! Oh, that man would fall on his knees! Oh, that man could behold My beauty!

I AM—THERE IS NO OTHER.

I AM the Center of everything.
I AM the Source of all Life.

I AM THAT I AM[64]—THERE IS NO OTHER.

Don't think for a moment, don't entertain the thought that man can do anything. He is needy, helpless, empty.

I AM the One who fills up the empty places, who satisfies all needs, who repairs what is broken, who heals what is sick, who mends what is torn, who feeds what is hungry, who finds what is lost, who gives Light where there is darkness. It is I.

I AM HE—THERE IS NO OTHER.

Oh yes, I have servants who take of Me and give out as I instruct, who drink of Me and refresh the weary souls, who taste of Me and feed the hungry. Yes, these are My brethren, My sisters, My friends. We are One. These shed abroad My gifts at My bidding. They step carefully, they look closely, they listen attentively.

They don't forge ahead as one bulldozing a trail. No, they watch, they wait, they search until they see the path I have for them, the one I have trodden, where My feet have been.[65] Yes, these are the ones who are useful in My Kingdom. These are the ones who will see what has been hidden from view, obscured for a time.

As My little ones follow Me on the path, I lead them with care, I hold their hands, I show them the way. They have no fear, no worries, no concerns.

> THEY KNOW I AM THERE, THAT I AM HE, AND THAT THERE IS NO OTHER.

What It's All About

It's not about
how much one can amass or even how much you
can give away.

It's not about
credit or loans or debts.

It's not about
having the perfect job or enough recreation.

It's about My precious ones, My faithful servants,

>   allowing My plans to be utmost in their lives,
>
>   giving of their time and money as I see fit,
>
>   not being swayed by opinions or wants,
>
>   > being wholly directed by My Spirit
>   >
>   > > to be reservoirs of Love, of Power,
>   >
>   > not content to be like the world.

Not as a Mere Reflection

Remember that it was *I* who called you, and it is *I* who will bring you to the place you need to be.

Oh, don't get restless.

Don't be impatient.

I am working.

Yes, but it is a work like no other you've seen.

When you come out on the other side, My Glory, My Countenance, My Face, they will see, not as a mere reflection, not as a vague shadow. No!

I WILL SO CONSUME YOU AND SATURATE YOUR BEING THAT OTHERS WILL THROW UP THEIR HANDS AND SHOUT, "GLORY!"

Yes, you will be My hands and My feet. You will walk among those called out as I have ordained you to walk.

Acknowledge My Presence in you.
Acknowledge My workings in you.

Just Love Them

Oh, My child, treat your children like I do you. Show them My heart of compassion.

Be an expression of Me.

Reflect My goodness. Reflect My Love.

Reflect Me.

Oh, don't speak of their sin. Don't voice it. Don't talk about their faults. Treat them the way you want to be treated. Let Me be in charge of molding their character. You can't mold anything. Don't voice your frustrations. Turn to Me. Yes, Look to Me. Listen to Me. I'm the only One, as I have said, who knows what they need.

Oh, take My Hand.

Don't ignore Me. Just give in and see Me work on their little hearts. Oh, you won't believe the transformation if you just love them, if you just help them, if you just hold them up to Me—to do as I please. Oh, you won't believe what I can do.

Just let go, My child.

That Secret Place

Don't look as others look. For your eyes will see My salvation. Your eyes will see that place of rest, that sanctuary, that abiding place.

Stay sheltered under My Wings.

Learn to abide in that secret place. Learn *to* rest under the Shadow of The Almighty.[66]

Take refuge from each storm. Don't venture out. Don't remove yourself through fear or worry. Don't step out into the rushing wind, for I will shield you.

It is *I* who will keep you.

As I have kept you before, I will keep you again. Just look to Me.

I AM your Refuge.

Center up as you have before. Center up.

Don't be distracted by those around you. Don't look or listen when they speak. Don't set your eyes on them as they try to take your eyes off Me. Don't let them steal your time and attention. Focus on *Me* and what *I'm* doing.

> Focus on *My* Word and *My* ways, on *My* will for you each moment.

So many distractions vie for your time, yet it is *Mine,* Mine to do with as I wish.

Met by the Living God

Oh, make no assumptions. Ascertain in the Spirit the necessary course of action. Do not continue to set a course in the dark without hearing My voice. For *My voice* and *only My voice* will instruct you correctly. *My eyes* and *only My eyes* will be a clear window for your soul. *My hands* and *only My hands* will shape the events necessary for this plan of mine to continue. *My ears* and *only My ears* will enable you to hear that faint stirring as it rises to a crescendo.

Take what I've given you. Rise and walk. Be that precious one I've called you to be. As *the man at the Gate Beautiful*,[67] waiting for a response to his need, calls out to man for help—He is met by the Living God—I AM. So it will be with many as I begin to shake them. The scales will fall off their eyes. Like blind Bartimaeus, they will jump to their feet, rising in glory to behold One who is altogether lovely. They will leave their rags behind to be trampled in the crowd, left in the dust. They have cried out in their need, "Son of David, have mercy on me,"[68] and I have heard them.

No, it will not be long. Now, the day is at hand. The very hour of My return is approaching swiftly, but it will not be as they suppose. My unveiling will not be as they have imagined, for they have imagined an illusion. They want to look with their naked eye to see what cannot be seen in their realm.

They believe I will pierce the darkness, and yes, I will, but My work will be to penetrate the cloud—the shadow of deceit that's been over their minds' eye. Oh yes, the shadow has been lifted off many, and there are many, many more to come. Watch in the Spirit. Wait in My realm. See them change. What a work I am doing in their hearts! What an awesome work I am doing even now!

Isn't It Enough?

Whatever the times, whatever the days and the season, whatever the assignment, oh, My hand will lead you. Isn't it enough that I'm there? Isn't it enough that I watch over you and keep you in My hand, that I nestle you in a safe place?

Isn't it enough?

Haven't I provided all that you need? Haven't I laid it at your feet? Can't you see it? Can't you see all My provision? Can't you feel My touch? Can't you sense My Presence?

Isn't it enough?

Stop looking outside.

I Am within.

Oh, can't you see? Open your eyes! Encompassed about are you. Oh yes, surrounded on all sides. Oh, I've seen. Yes, I've heard all that you've placed before Me.

Isn't it enough that I know?
Isn't it enough that I hear?

Must you know the outcome to trust Me? Must you see the path to feel secure? Isn't it enough that I am there to hold your hand, to carry you?

OH, STEP INTO MY ARMS, AND LET ME HOLD YOU CLOSE! LET MINE BE THE VOICE THAT CHEERS YOUR SOUL, THAT COMFORTS YOUR HEART, THAT BRINGS YOU PEACE!

At Arm's Length

Oh, My child, when will you learn? Oh, when will you come to Me, call on Me, lean on Me? When will you stop chasing after what I've created, what I've fashioned, and seek Me?

> OH, I LONG TO SHARE MY TREASURES WITH YOU!

[In my spirit, I saw a child crawl up in his daddy's lap. The daddy had a gift for him that they were to open as the child settled in on His lap.]

I long to hold you and give you those special gifts I have waiting for you, but you stay away. You won't come close. You won't enjoy Me.

You keep waiting for Me to reach out and hand it to you at arm's length. I do this—oh yes, I must—but it's not My heart's desire. For if I did not reach out, reach down, and hand My children their toys; if I actually waited for them to run and jump into My lap empty-handed just to be near Me, just to hear Me whisper in their ear, just to know I'm there; so many of My children would go away pouting, discouraged, dismayed wondering why I didn't love them, why I don't care, so My righteous right arm reaches out to meet them.

I allow them to play in the corner with their toys to hide from Me and have their fun, but when they get lonely, when their toys break, when they get hungry, when they get tired,

SHARED BY LAURA WILCOTT

when they fall down and scrape their knee, then they will look around, they'll call My Name, they'll come searching for Me—even though I was there all along. They were just too busy to notice, too busy to care.

Step Into Your Calling

The time has come when nothing in you that is not of Me can stay. I want to wash you and fill you up with Me. I desire to cleanse this vessel for My purposes. Do not say it will be a long time, for it will not! Do not say, "I'm learning." For you will not learn this. It will be given to you, so don't stand there waiting, for My Spirit will do it now—no waiting! You will see it now. You will see the change. You will witness the transformation take place even now. My purposes will stand. I will have My way in you.

> I AM LORD.
>
> HONOR ME AS LORD.
>
> YIELD TO ME AS LORD.

Be now that instrument of Mine that I can use. Yes, you have been unyielded in some ways, but I will change that. I will cause your spirit to rise up and be master over your soul. You will see it come to pass quickly. Do not worry. Do not be concerned, for I wish to point My children to the Father. You are just the vessel, so don't be concerned by what you see. Let Me minister through you as I see fit. Don't put the focus on you. Don't turn your eyes onto yourself.

> **Just walk as I lead you.**
>
> **The way has been prepared.**

The timing is now. You will step into and walk in your calling, even now. Oh, yes, it will be Me who accomplishes this,

Shared by Laura Wilcott

so be at peace. *Acknowledge Me in all your ways, and I will direct your paths.*[69]

Don't be timid, for the Lion of Judah who indwells you will rise up! He will have His way!

Their "Holy" Ambitions

As an undernourished plant begins to grow as it is nursed back to health, so is it with My children in these days. They have been sickly, wilted, limp, unable to hold even themselves up. They have been malnourished because their root has been anchored in sand.

The sand, as I have told you, is a product of man's work. As a sand dune holds not the sustenance necessary to enable life to flourish, so man's work is devoid of the elements necessary to nurture My people in the growth process. Their growth will be stunted.

Look at a sand dune, then consider man's work on My behalf. I did not say, "*My* work," for *My* work is as the grandest mountains, the luscious forests, the most fertile valleys. When I work in and through man, he can but stare in wonder at the things I do. He can but fall down in awe and praise at My indescribable wisdom and grace on his behalf.

No, I am not in many of their "glorious" plans—plans they've conceived of their own—futile plans. No, I am not in their constant strivings. There is so much that man does in My Name, for My sake, in My honor that is but dung. They wish to succeed in all their "holy" ambitions, never giving thought to My direction.

Their desires rule them. Their pride propels them. They love to believe My hand is in their projects, their programs, their missions, yet they have not consulted Me.

They have not waited on instructions. They have not been still in My Presence. They rely on tradition. They rely on opinions. They rely on a vote!

Where are they? Where are they who will stop where they are, who will fall down on their knees and repent? For all *their filthy rags*[70] they've been carrying are but a burden, a weight that has been slowing them down.

> *Come to Me, all you who labor and are heavy laden, and I will give you rest. Take My yoke upon you and learn from Me, for I am gentle and lowly in heart, and you will find rest for your souls. For My yoke is easy and My burden is light.*[71]

Oh, let go of the weight you've been carrying, for anything that's not of Me is a burden.

[*How do I let go?*]

YOU ABIDE IN MY PRESENCE. YOU SWIM IN MY OCEAN. YOU JUMP INTO MY RIVER. YOU STAND UNDER MY WATERFALL.

You take *every thought captive to the obedience of Christ*.[72] You cease your futile efforts of self and know that I AM. I will build a wall around you—an impenetrable wall. Those desires you have will no longer plague you.

You are free.

Walk in that freedom.

I WOULD HAVE YOU COME TO THE WATERS TO DRINK![73]

Blindfolded

Don't worry yourself in the least about those who walk in darkness seeking to instruct you. They are as a child blindfolded, bumping into things along the way, groping in the night.

> Do not judge. Do not confront except by My Spirit. Do not testify of yourself. Do not make a way for your words. I'll do that!

Stand your ground in meekness. Only your eyes will see what I have laid out before you. Only your ears will hear My instructions for your soul. Not one part of My message to you will be given to another. They will not know what I say to you, so don't be concerned that they do not believe. Do not be anxious that they do not see, for I will cause those called to believe, called to see, to walk into that with no effort.

Let go! The very work you desire to see in them is My work, yet you continue to hold on wanting to help. I already told you that I need no help!

An Awesome Work

You are to shine as a star shines at night. You are to be a beacon of Light for those who have lost their way.

[*I thought Jesus was the Beacon of Light.*]

Yes, and He, the *Light of life* is in you—so shine!

Ask now for My Spirit to draw those in darkness. Abundant, abundant is My mercy upon you. Abundant, abundant is My grace. Many who are blind will see. Many who cannot see even now will walk into the Light that I give you.

Don't extinguish that Light.

Let it burn brightly.

Hold on to that which I've given you! Press into that which I've prepared for you!

Be still and see My Spirit move into every area of your life.

Don't be shocked at the transformation that will take place, for even now, a great transformation is being wrought in your soul—apart from any effort of yours, apart from any plan you could conceive.

OH, WHAT A GLORIOUS CHANGE I HAVE WROUGHT!

Glorify Me, for I am doing a work,

an awesome work!

That Gentle Nudge

Take a look at those precious ones around you. Examine closely their every need.

> OH, HOW THEY NEED A GENTLE TOUCH, A COMFORTING VOICE, AN ENCOURAGING SMILE!

I'll be what you cannot be. I'll reach out and touch them as you long to.

Yes, you're beginning to see what I have in store for you. That gentle disposition is awaiting you as you rest in My goodness. For each moment is but an opportunity to draw you in closer, deeper into My peace. Yes, your agenda has to go for My peaceful Presence to pervade. Yes, you'll have to be flexible, not holding on stubbornly to your plan for the moment. You must flow with My Spirit, or you will be frustrated.

Planning is good, schedules are fine, but they must yield to My leading at each and every moment. Give up the plan, throw out the schedule if My Spirit says, "Stop, turn, and follow Me." The woman with the issue of blood[74] did not fit in the schedule; she was not part of man's plan, yet her need was satisfied, her desires fulfilled because the plan wasn't the priority—it was obedience.

So next time you have a goal, an idea of how your day should go, remember that gentle nudge that still, small voice is not to be ignored, for I will not lead you astray. I will show you the way of the Father, the lighted path, the sure and steady course. No time will be lost, no priority of Mine mishandled as you yield to My gentle leading as you respond to My quiet instructions moment by moment.

What Patience! What Love!

Reserved for My Glory are you. Yes, I see you and know how needy you are. Yes, I am well acquainted with your faults. I know what's inside man, what his heart is capable of, yet I choose these very vessels to display My Glory in the Face of Christ.

Only by My grace will you stand. Only by My hand will you yield. Only through My eyes will you see. Don't look at your sin—only Me. Keep your eyes fixed, focused on Me. Created, even molded, yes, intricately handcrafted for this hour are you.

Oh yes, you see the stubble and say, "Why, why the imperfections? Why the struggles?" You can't imagine how you, of all people, could be used. "Why do you put up with me?" you ask. Yet day after day, week after week, month after month, even year after year, I am here holding your hand, helping you up, making you stand.

"What love! What patience! What grace!" you say. And yes, these seem so clear to those who have been shown they are needy and vile and wretched. The others have been blinded for a time, trapped in their own selfish pride, lost in their own arrogance, not heeding My voice—deaf, mute, blind.

But these will be brought out of the darkness into the Light. These who have been blind will see. They will see Me in all My Glory as I reveal to them their desperate state, as I show them the pit they are in, as I reach out and take their hand.

As I bring them out, they will shout My praises, they will stand in amazement at My grace, they will be in awe of My mercy just as you have been.

So don't think it strange that I use such vessels, for that is how I work—*for My Glory!*

As Fast as You Can Listen

Open up to Me more. Turn your ear to Me more often. Yes, walk where it is light before you. Don't step into confusion. Don't worry about My leading anymore. You can follow. I can lead with no difficulty.

> **Stop looking to man to be your guide,**
>
> **your instructor,**
>
> **your confidant.**

You can and will follow Me easily, so don't be swayed from the lighted path set out for you plainly. I already told you I have much, much more to give you, but you must listen. I can change you as fast as you can listen.

Take the Word and eat it. My Word of Life. *All that eat of it will live.*

> I WOULD THAT YOU WOULD HEARKEN UNTO MY VOICE NIGHT AND DAY, EVERY PASSING MOMENT.
>
> You must focus on Me!

Out of Your Comfort Zone

You've been given a gift. Use it for My glory. Employ it to My satisfaction.[75] Don't wait on others to be obedient. You are not called to wait.

You must be a light in a dark place, a candle whose flame does not flicker, burning consistently while others may fail.

Don't remain in the shadows any longer.

I have a work for you to work.

Yes, you must learn to speak only when I instruct you to speak, yet now is the time for you to begin to operate in the giftings you have been given.

You must step out of your comfort zone and rely on Me to lead you. Fall onto My grace. You will begin to hear your instructions step by step. Press into Me every moment. Press into Me for direction, for your every response.

Do not speak rashly. I will tell you what to say. You have been prepared for this moment. You have been hewn out of the Rock for this time. You need to not follow others' instruction—only Mine.

I'm the Gift!

Don't get distracted. It's My work. Go about your business. Keep your mind on what I have you to do. You are elevating the work above Me when your focus gets off Me.

Enjoy Me in it all.

Enjoy Me in the triumphs. Enjoy Me in the success. Be consumed with Me, not with what I hand you. Don't take My gifts, then run off to enjoy them alone.

I'm the gift! I'm your delight!

I'm your satisfaction!

Don't get confused. Things won't satisfy, and you know it. Remember Me in it all. Let's walk together, just you and Me.

Like a refreshing rain on the parched ground, like dew of a morning, am I to a weary soul. Oh, you're weary and need a drink of water. You're tired and need rest.

I am the Rest that you seek. I am that Refreshing for your soul.

I am that drink of Life-giving water.

Drink of Me.

Oh, drink of Me.

Shared by Laura Wilcott

Gentle, I am gentle with My children. My tender mercies, My compassions, they fail not.

Illusions of Control

You must die to any illusions you have of maintaining a sense of control.

>**I will control your destiny.**
>
>**You will submit to My control.**

Many believe they are in control. Many think their destiny is in their control, but they are blind to the truth. I hold them in My hand and direct them as I see fit.

I fashion them as a vessel for My purposes, which they cannot fully understand. I see what lies ahead and prepare the way for their feet to walk. No, they are not in control. My purposes are greater than they can fathom, higher than they can grasp.

>**I teach them My way as they are ready.**
>
>**I show them the path as they yield to Me.**

Don't stand back from My road, seeking to make your own way.

>**MY WAY IS THE ONLY WAY.**

Every other path leads to destruction. Any other path forged by man leads only to sorrow and regrets.

Shared by Laura Wilcott

The Whys of Life

Oh, My child, rest. All that has been established is set in place for a specific plan. It is not up to man to realize that plan—just to yield.

> I AM THE GREAT ORCHESTRATOR OF MY DESIGN.

I see every detail and carry it out to perfection. I ordain events just as they occur, but man believes in chance.

> **Nothing is a mistake.**
>
> **Everything is necessary.**
>
> I AND ONLY I KNOW THE WHYS OF LIFE.

Some events are shaped to make men stronger. Some are to lift them up, while others are as a purifying fire refining the soul.

The Picture Many Paint of Me

Yes, man knows nothing, sees nothing, perceives nothing but by My Spirit. He can only grope along in darkness even if that darkness is his religious fantasy—believing that he pleases Me with his many activities, his constant striving to please.

For I desire obedience rather than sacrifice[76] and a contrite heart rather than their many offerings of self. What an affront to My nature! I do not need nor want what they give. They cannot earn My Love. They cannot pay for it and hope I don't see their hearts—the very things they hide. They believe I don't see. They think they have fooled Me, the One who fashions them. Oh, I don't want their many gifts of self and possessions—their empty works. I just want them.

> I AM ALTOGETHER LOVELY, READY TO TAKE THEM TO A PLACE OF REST, READY TO CLOTHE THEM WITH MY RAIMENT,[77] READY TO WASH THEM IN MY RIVER, READY TO FILL THEM WITH MY LOVE.

I don't look to man to perform, but that is the picture many paint of Me. They see Me as One watching from the sidelines, cheering them on in their many endeavors to please, patting them on the back for their glory. Oh no, I will not share My glory with them. I will be glorified. They will come naked, empty, alone—stripped of all they held dear—kneeling at My feet, then they will realize I AM *all* they need.

> WHEN I FILL THEM, WHEN I WASH THEM, WHEN I CLOTHE THEM, WHEN I TOUCH THEM, THEN THEY WILL SEE MY BEAUTY FOR THEIR ASHES, MY GLORY FOR THEIR SHAME, MY GOODNESS AND ONLY MINE.

They will see that their efforts to be were futile, empty, shallow, worthless! They will behold My Glory in that day, and what a day it will be!

Carried Swiftly

[*I cried out, "I don't like myself. Spare me from myself, Lord!"*]

I already have.

Precious, how absolutely precious it is to Me for My servants, My friends, to fall on My grace. My little ones who wait patiently for Me to mold them gently into a creation for My glory walk out that plan I have for them with ease.

They do not strive nor strain against the current of My Love. They do not heap up a dam, as some do, that stops the flow of My Spirit.

Let Me carry you swiftly. It need not be as you suppose. My Spirit knows no boundaries, has no limitations.

You are in My control.

Only yield.

Stay in My peaceful Presence, bask in My Love, then it will be as you desire. You will walk unhindered. I'm taking you to that place.

Enter in.

Shared by Laura Wilcott

The Voice of the Accuser

Oh, My child, your ways are not My ways, neither are your thoughts Mine. Cease your attempts to control your spouse. Give Me your children. They are already in My hands. They are already in My tender care.

Yes, encourage them all. Yes, speak good things into their lives. Yes, share hope, the hope that you see of the change I have wrought and will effect in their lives.

Don't be the voice of the *accuser*. Don't give him a word, an action, a moment. Don't usher him to their hearts. Usher in peace, usher in hope, usher in Love—My Love.

Hold their hand and jump into My river.

Ask a lot of questions. Share with them your struggles. Don't speak ill of *your spouse* in their presence. Lift him up. Show them the good—what they have to be thankful for, why they should rejoice.

Oh yes, I'll bring in that good, sweet, precious harmony you desire in your home, in your loved ones. Only enter in by My grace. Lead the way.

Be a reflection of Me.

My child, it's so much better than what you've tasted. You'll see that sweet Presence entering into every area of your life, your family, your home. Oh yes, I have victory in store for you all, sweet victory. Just walk into it. It has been placed before you. It has been set at your feet.

Remember

Remember the times I've carried you. Remember the many times I've held your hand when you were too weak to stand. Remember My goodness. Remember My gracious hand in your affairs. Remember the good words I've spoken over your life.

> Call to mind My excellencies, My abundant provision, My great and awesome Power.

Be still before Me in My holiness. Don't hasten to speak. Take care with your words.

For as the sun rises over the horizon, so is My faithfulness. As the stars in the sky cannot be counted, so are My mercies toward those who call on My Name, who hope in Me.

Oh, I am rich in My mercies toward the many! They hope in what they cannot see, but those who see delight in Me.

> Carry on in My *river of delights*.[78]

Don't forget to be refreshed in My fountain. Don't trudge up a hill weighed down by concerns of this life.

Enter in and soar as the eagles, high above the hills and valleys. Open up your wings. For My wind will carry you to new heights.

His Awesome Plans

What exactly did you think life was going to be like? Did you visualize a life of ease, comfort, serenity? Could you have foreseen this? Would you have wanted to? No! My children do not know, cannot see My plans in all their glory, for My plans are glorious. They are perfect. They are necessary.

If man were in charge of the plans for their lives, My glorious grace they could not see, My sweet goodness they would not appreciate. They would be so full they would not know they had a need. They would not see their helpless, wicked state. They would not come to Me. They would not call out in their distress for Me to touch them, heal them, mend their broken hearts.

They could not fathom My Redemptive Love unless they had been unlovely. They could not see My Gracious Hand unless they'd had a need. They could not know My Glorious Presence unless they had felt alone, forsaken, lost. They could not fathom the glory of My plan unless theirs had come to naught, but when they come—finally come—kneeling in desperation, oh, what joy is theirs! Oh, what peace! Oh, what glory is theirs!

For they have walked in the valley of the shadow of death and now perceive Life. They have cried in their grief and now rejoice in joy inexpressible!

They have been blind, and now they see! They have been lame, and now they walk! They have been deaf, and now they hear! Oh, the troubles, the trials are so needful! The mountains must be crossed, the valleys must be endured, the rivers must be forged for one to fully appreciate the destination for one to throw up his hands and shout, "I'm home! I'm home! I'm finally home!"

Keep your eyes on the moment. Don't set your gaze in the distance, for My Kingdom is now! My workings are today!

Surpassing Man's Ability to Reason

Yes, I'll walk you through the door of Love. Yes, I'll hold your hand as you step into My Love. My Love is so much deeper, more fulfilling than what you have imagined. It surpasses man's ability to reason.

Enter in by My grace. Enter in through worship, through abiding.

Cleave to Me.

Fill up in My Presence.

Be full for the task. Be filled to overflowing.

My Love will overflow out of your being.

So rejoice, for you will see it. It will come to pass. Nothing can separate you from My Love. Nothing can keep you down when I choose to raise you up. Nothing can stop the course of My Spirit.

Flow with My Spirit.

Do not strain against My wind. Do not plant your feet in the sands of fear.

Pick up and fly.

Pick up and soar.

Soar to new heights in the Spirit. Nothing can stop your ascent as you keep your eyes on Me.

The Potter, Not the Clay

Determined am I to make a way before you. Settled am I for the task of molding you *as a potter molds his clay*[79] into a beautiful vessel. He has complete control over the process, the design, the outcome. He wonders not what kind of vessel he'll make. He has each detail planned out. He does not consult the clay. He doesn't look to it to help in the creation of the vessel. He doesn't depend on the clay to do anything. He is the craftsman. He has a plan.

Oh, My children think they have so much to do with the outcomes they see! They truly believe they are assisting Me in My endeavors! I allow them to be blind to their helplessness for a season. *I let them gloat in their pride. I let them strut,*[80] but not for long. For their strutting days are over. No more, no more will I stand back and let them get the glory.

I will intervene. I will step into their mapped-out plans, their well-thought-out endeavors and show them they are nothing. I plan to raise up those whose eyes are opened, those who see the Light of My Countenance, who behold My Face in the light of their humble state. They will perceive the real happenings.

> THEY WILL KNOW IT'S ME WHO PICKS THEM UP AND TURNS THEM AROUND, WHO STARTS THEM ON THEIR WAY, WHO EMBRACES THEM.

I AM He.

As a Man Who Guards a City

Blessings and honor are reserved for My children who take special care with My Word, whether spoken in their ear or revealed from Scripture.

Take My Word as a treasure. Hold it close, for *I watch over My Word to perform it.*[81] I keep watch as a man who guards a city. Vigilantly do I keep every word. Faithfully do I enact every stroke of the pen, every jot, every tittle.

No one knows how I perform My great and awesome deeds in righteousness. No one can see the full extent as it is spoken. I keep My good Word.

Only My servants who can hear and obey explicitly will be of much use in My Kingdom. Only these faithful children will sit and dine around My table while the others will have a time of testing, trial, and fire. Each one must come to the place of complete surrender to My will, My ways, My workings.

Nothing else will satisfy Me.

Driving a Wedge

What is it that you keep doing? What's the benefit of all your effort? It's just driving a wedge between you and those you try to control.

> Oh, if you could only see how perfect My work is on their behalf, how I am molding your loved ones as I am you!

You slow up the growth *in you, not them,* when you try to do My work for Me. You're saying you can do it better every time you meddle in My business every time you launch out without Me seeking to do what I can only do in them.

Let go! The very work you desire to see in them is *My work,* yet you continue to hold on wanting to help.

> I already told you that I need no help!

Oh yes, it is like you've seen. It is, as one, preparing something in the kitchen following a recipe and having a toddler climb up in the way. They cannot see that they are hindering the very work they are so eager for you to carry out. They do not understand that you do not need their help, that you are more than capable of doing what you set out to do. You long for them to go play so you can work without cleaning up their messes.

> Yes, My child, it's time.
> Enter in.

Shared by Laura Wilcott

As a Treasure to Be Guarded

You need to take care with the visions I give you. You need to take care with the things I tell you. They are a precious treasure to be guarded, kept safe until the proper time.

As this baby must grow in the womb unto maturity, for the proper time to come forth, so is My Word sent for the saints. You must guard your words and make no assumptions. You need only to follow My voice.

No matter what you receive from My Spirit, I want you to take it as a treasure and offer it up to Me in praise. You are to carry My Word to those ordained to hear. Take care how you handle this precious treasure of Mine. I will direct you into the Light.

Take care with every step.

Yes, take care.

Mapped Out Carefully

Didn't I say you would know My leading step by step? Haven't I made a way for you already? Each and every step you are to take has been mapped out carefully. You don't need to be so concerned about how or when it will occur.

You just need to enjoy the journey.

Just press into Me, and I will direct you. I will order your steps.

BE AT PEACE FOR THE JOURNEY.

Wait on My Spirit to direct you. Don't forge ahead. Don't be led at all by your mind. *Only My Spirit knows the way.*

Empty yourself moment by moment into My will for you. Yes, you are beginning to see how to walk by the Spirit. Yes, you will see even clearer the path you are to take.

It will shine ever brighter

as you empty yourself

into Me.

Shared by Laura Wilcott

I AM Tomorrow

I AM *the Light of life.*

My children who walk by My Light have no fear of stumbling. They do not fear what man fears. For much of man's fear comes from the unknown. My servants of Light know I have them carefully in My hand. They know I direct their steps. They know there is no cause to fear, for I know tomorrow.

I AM TOMORROW.

If you could see that I AM, your fears would dispel, for I am the answer to everything—every concern, every worry, every fear.

I AM THAT I AM.[82] THERE IS NO OTHER.[83]

When will you learn? I am your bread,[84] and I am your water. Come to Me and be full.

Jars of Clay

Attend to the assignments you're given. Be quick to respond when My Spirit speaks. Don't be slothful. Each and every task, each and every assignment, is laid out before you not only to affect My plan but to produce an effect in you also. I am interested in molding you, step by step, into that creation that I have ordained.

> NO, YOU WON'T GET THE GLORY. NO, YOU WON'T SEEK THE PRAISE BECAUSE YOU WILL SEE AND CLEARLY UNDERSTAND THAT IT HAS ALL BEEN A WORK OF GRACE AND NONE OTHER.

This work of grace that you see in others has come about by My hand, so don't give glory to another. Don't think that it has anything to do with the will of man. His power has not produced any of the change that you see, for man, in and of himself, is powerless. For My servant has spoken, "*We have this treasure in jars of clay to show that this all-surpassing power is from God and not from us.*"[85]

Yes, in My wisdom, I have ordained this so.

Mercy on Them All

I have fashioned man as I see fit. I have made him weak, helpless, vile, wicked.

> It is not a mistake that they need a Savior. It is not an accident—not happenstance—that man is trapped in his sin.

Do you think that I am subject to the will of the devil, a created being? Do you think that he had anything to do with My divine purposes, My excellent plans? What nonsense! Man is so blind to My Power, My Wisdom!

Does a clockmaker worry at night whether one of his creations will circumvent his plans for his factory, whether one of his clocks will steal away of its own will and take over production? What a ridiculous thought! One would say, "How absurd!" Yet My people, My very offspring, believe such notions about their adversary.

They actually imagine that I am at the whim of one that My hands have fashioned, that I would create one that could mess up My plans! What utter nonsense!

My Word to them is this. "For God has bound up all in disobedience; so that He may show mercy to all. Oh, the depth of the riches, both of the wisdom and knowledge of God! How unsearchable are His judgments and unfathomable His ways!"[86]

In the Midst of Despair

As the sands on the seashore wash up then are gone, so are those fleeting plans that enter a man's heart to consume him. If only he would yield himself without reserve to My plans, he would find himself standing on a Rock, not knowing how he got there. So many succumb to the tide as it ebbs and flows, but My servants are set securely, as a rock that juts out from the sand is anchored on the rock.

Call to order that which is out of place in your thinking. How did you think that you could justify planning your life for Me? Would it not have been better to say, *"Be it to me according to Your will"* and rested in My goodness. You see, man sees the pain, trials, and troubles and wants to run the other way. He cannot fathom how the valley he is to enter is placed there for his good, how the walk he sees with his natural eyes can have such far-reaching benefits, but *I see!*

If he would but throw himself onto Me with all his aspirations and rest in My perfect plan, then he will see the sunrise behind the dark clouds. In an instant, I can open his eyes to see My radiant Glory in the midst of his despair.

He must look to Me when his load seems weary, for I have said, *"Come unto Me all you who are weary and heavy laden, and I will give you rest!"*[87]

MY SWEET REST WILL KEEP YOU.

JUST LOOK TO ME!

"Not My Will but Thine!"

Whether or not I speak to your heart, whether or not I answer your prayer, whether or not I give you your desires, I AM. No soul that calls out to Me will be unsatisfied. Yes, your temporal desires may not all be fulfilled. Yes, you may need to walk a road you did not want. Yes, you will need to die a death so ordained. But as you come out on the other side—as you step into My realm, into My blessing—what joy will be yours!

You will see that I AM, that I was, and that I will be all you need. Don't look around, but set your eyes on My grace, on My goodness, on My mercy.

I AM YOUR EXCEEDING GREAT REWARD,[88] NOT WHAT YOU SEEK.

No more asking for the things you desire. Nor more seeking the things you desire. My will *will* be the focus of your mind. My thoughts, My plans, My purposes will stand.

Seek only My will. Have no agenda. *"Not my will but Thine!"*[89] will be your cry.

That Spark, That Fire, That Blaze

I have deposited within you a treasure *for My glory*. I have set you upon your feet *for My glory*. I have carefully handcrafted you, taking care with every detail *for My glory*. You needn't think that you had anything to do with it. Brush aside any thoughts you may have of taking center stage.

STAY IN THE SHADOW OF MY WINGS.

Abide, as you are, in that secret place waiting on Me to shine, for I will shine through you. You needn't worry or concern yourself with how you will muster up that strength, that resolve, that passion. Just as I have come in the past, just as I have met you where you were, I will meet you again.

OH, MAN LOOKS TO HIMSELF WHEN I, AND ONLY I, HAVE WHAT HE NEEDS.

He is deluded into thinking that *that* spark, *that* fire, *that* blaze he looks for will be kindled by something deep within him. And yes, it will be kindled, and yes, it will burn, but *I* have deposited it. *I* have placed it. *I* have called it forth!

COME FORTH! ARISE! SHINE! FOR YOUR LIGHT HAS COME, AND THE GLORY OF THE LORD HAS RISEN UPON YOU![90]

Just Whisper My Name

    Abide.

        Abide.

            Abide.[91]

Center up into Me. Yes, you see, you hear, and you speak, but that's not enough, for only in My peaceful Presence will you ever find that rest you are searching for. I can't take you to that place unless you abide.

    Abide in peace.

        Abide in worship.

            Abide in prayer.

Talk to Me more than you talk to the children. Listen to Me more than to those around you.

Take time for Me. I'll do your housework with you. I'll go on your errands with you. I'll even be there with every step as you walk through those rough moments that come crashing into your peaceful abode.

    Just call out to Me.

        Just whisper My Name.

            Oh, I AM there!

Shared by Laura Wilcott

Your Partner, Your Lover, Your Friend

No, don't go it alone. Don't trudge up that mountain alone. Oh, when I take the road with a man, his steps are not cumbersome, his load is not weary, his face is not downcast!

> For I make the way as a path strewn with flowers, as a footbridge beside a waterfall, as a set of stairs in a palace.

No one can take My road with Me and keep their eyes too long on the path. For I am too lovely to ignore. I am too awesome to forget. I am too priceless to brush aside.

> Oh, let Me be your Partner, your Lover, your Friend!
>
> I am here!
>
> Oh, take My hand!
>
> We'll walk together, just you and Me.

Won't it be sweet, holding hands in My garden? Won't it be grand, waltzing to My music?

When you see yourself as I AM, I will be glorified.

SEE ME AS I AM

According to a predetermined plan laid out in fine detail will you walk in the Kingdom. Don't think that I am watching from the sidelines. Don't imagine Me on a throne, for My throne is your heart. My dwelling place is within you. My self is yours. Don't wonder where I am, for I AM your very breath.

Man, in all his grand ideas, sees Me as a judge and not a friend, as a master and not a husband, as a king and not a father.

> OH, I WOULD THAT MY CHILDREN WOULD SEE ME AS I AM!

For their imaginations of who I am keep them alone. They need only to call My Name. They need only to whisper a prayer. They need only to open their eyes, as I allow them, and they will see that I have always been there, that I have been by their side all along.

> OH, MAN WOULD LIKE TO BELIEVE THAT I AM THERE TO PRAISE THEM WHEN THEY STAND AND JUDGE THEIR BROTHER WHEN HE FALLS! OH, I AM SO MUCH MORE!

I am not what they think. I AM their true Reflection—not of the dross, for that will burn away, not of their position, for that will change, not of their personality, for that can be molded. No! I AM who they are. They are Me.

> WE ARE ONE.[92]

To Quench a Thirst

Like a river that flows continually from the throne of God is My Word to you in Power and Glory. I will reveal Myself to you in the coming days. Oh, My child, you cannot see as yet the rich blessing in store for you as you abide!

Stay in My river.

No, don't listen to that inferior voice that will come to steal you away. Take care to discern the voices that vie for your attention.

Don't make assumptions.

Try them in light of who I AM.

Test them.

Rest in Me, for I am working even now to perfect you. As water quenches the thirst, so you will quench the thirst of those weary from a long journey. Tired and restless are My people. They need a drink.

Wait on Me, for I will perform that which concerns Me.

Step in My steps.

Wait on Me.

Learn to not forge ahead. Learn to wait on direction and instruction. This is very important.

Shared by Laura Wilcott

Be Aflame!

Hide in the cleft of the Rock. Take shelter under My Wings. Stay anchored, secured *to the Rock*.[93] As the wind picks up and you see the tempest about you,

> keep your eyes fixed on Me,
>> keep your mind stayed on Me,[94]
>>> keep your hope set on Me.

BURN BRIGHTLY. BE AFLAME WITH THOSE WORDS I HAVE PUT ON YOUR LIPS. RISE UP! STAND.

You are in a place ordained by My Spirit, called forth from the womb for this time. Oh, you need not worry or concern yourself with what I am preparing you for—just be!

Let the winds of change grow. Let them carry you forward, higher. Don't hold back. Press on. Set your face like a flint. Don't resist.

> BE EAGER.
>> SHINE.

OH, YES, STEP OUT, BUT STEP OUT IN LOVE! LAUNCH OUT BUT IN A RIVER OF PEACE! SAIL—YES, SAIL—BUT BE CARRIED ON WAVES OF JOY!

Enjoy the Ride

I want you to know that apart from My Spirit, apart from My workings in your life, you will see no fruit that will remain.[95] As you step out, I will make your footsteps secure.

> YOU WILL HEAR ONLY AS I ALLOW YOU TO HEAR. YOU WILL SEE ONLY AS I GIVE YOU VISION. YOU WILL WALK ONLY AS I DIRECT. YOU WILL STAND AS I HOLD YOU UP.

So don't be concerned about today and how it will unfold nor tomorrow, for I am well able to orchestrate the events that are ordained without any of your concern. Just relax. Take it easy. Give your brain a rest. I'll work everything out as I have planned. Oh, I'll cause the provision to be there. I'll make a way where there seems to be no other.

> [*I saw a foot step out into the air where there appeared to be nothing, but as it stepped, it was on something secure, even though it was invisible to the naked eye. You could see a shimmering of the air like the surface of something solid—like special effects.*]

Oh, trust Me and enjoy the ride. There is so much yet to see, so much to taste, so much to touch—so much!

Where You Veered Off

My child, what are you doing? Don't you know? Don't you see? Don't you understand that only by My way, only by My Spirit, only by My strength will your way be paved as with gold? Stop wasting My time in the bushes. Look to see where you lost your way, how you veered off the path.

Get back into what I am doing.

Jump back into My river.

Don't you see how futile, how empty your own endeavors come to be?

WHAT AN INFERIOR PATH MY CHILDREN CHOOSE!

WHAT NONSENSE THEY ENTER INTO DAY BY DAY!

I seek to show them a better way. Only in Me can your way be established. Only in My careful leading can you know the way laid out for you. Don't be consumed with fear, not knowing the way.

I AM THE WAY![96]

OH, BE AT PEACE!

Taking Possession

[*I asked the Lord, "Why do You seem to use some and not others in ministering?"*] Let Me teach you through everything: every encounter, every trial, every circumstance. Let Me train you—not just at meetings. Life is a classroom, but many of My children think it's just a playground. Yes, there's leisure time, but its purpose is to strengthen and restore you, not to pacify your carnal desires.

[*Then I saw in my mind's eyes a large circular classroom with chalkboards around the entire perimeter of the room. Everyone was seated facing outward toward the chalkboards. There were numerous instructors, each at a different chalkboard, each with a different audience, all teaching something different. There were preachers, ministers, rabbis, and priests of all different faiths with chalkboards full of instructions, all teaching to students attentive to what they were saying.*

Then Jesus came into the room and cleared His throat. A hush fell over the room as He put His things on the desk. It seemed obvious to all that this had actually been His classroom all along and not theirs—and He was taking possession!

The instructors quickly began to leave the room. Some paid little attention to Him and left as if offended. He held a pitcher, a clay pot of water. As some left the room, they held out their glass but hardly got a drop to drink because they wouldn't wait for Him to fill their glass before they left. Most of the students filed past Jesus just as quickly and responded in like manner.

A few instructors stayed behind with the few remaining students. All had turned away from the chalkboards to face Jesus. He approached each with His pitcher and began to fill their glasses. The water overflowed and spilled out onto the floor. The room began to fill up with water; then it began to rain inside the room. The water washed all the writing off all the chalkboards and drenched the ones who had stayed. All were rejoicing as they were bathed in this water.]

Religious Fantasies

You need to begin to direct your thoughts inward to your center. Let Me teach you what you do not know and cannot learn from man. Man has his own ideas he tries to fit into My truth. So few can take truth, My truth, as it is. They want to mold it and make it into their image of Me. They want to shape Me into their pretty picture, what feels good to their ignorant senses.

    I AM.

    Let Me show you who I AM.

Throw away your preconceived ideas, your religious fantasies of how I work. I want to teach you what eye cannot see, what ear cannot hear, what your mind cannot know. These lie. Your spirit knows Me.

Awake. Awake to who you are. Arise, My child, from the earth.

    Take up your wings.

    See as I see.

Reign in this life[97] as one who is eternal, knowing where you've come from and where you are going.

    I'll show you. Just look.

Shared by Laura Wilcott

STOP STRIVING. START RESTING.[98] THIS IS THE KEY.

As One Who Commands an Army

You have an anointing from the Holy One and know all things.[99] Let not your doubts come up as the waves on the shore. Let them not crash around you. Hold them in check with your words. Speak *as I spoke to the waves.*[100] Command as one commands an army. Act as one in charge.

Be even as I have called you to be, not tossed about with the winds and waves, not subject to those thoughts that try to steal your peace. For haven't I said that *I would keep him in perfect peace whose mind is stayed on Me,*[101] and haven't I done that, as you've called out to Me.

> Don't let your mind race.
>
> Arrest your thoughts.
>
> Take charge.

Oh, you've been placed in a position of authority, yet you act as one who gets her orders from those beneath in rank, from those who are supposed to get their orders from you as you speak from Me! I AM the Authority! I have set the ranks! I have established the authorities! Don't go against that which has been established.

Just listen as I command and do likewise. See your position! Know who commands! I even command the morning! The stars hold their place at My Word, the galaxies their positions! All heaven and earth operate and exist at My Word!

Don't you think I can keep you?

Shared by Laura Wilcott

Begin to Reign!

Today, begin to reign!

Enough time has been spent, too much, walking that inferior path, choosing those inferior words being less than has been ordained for you to be. Now is the time. The grace you need has been supplied. It is ample. You can walk, even now, as one set on high, as one reigning over a kingdom.

Don't hold back.

Don't hesitate.

Enter in!

Draw from Me.

Today is the day to set aside your agendas. They weary you. You see, they've been weighing you down. You see how they steal your peace, your joy, your rest.

Not by Might, Nor by Power

Can you trust Me? Am I faithful? Every moment, as you entrust yourself to Me, I will surely take care of that which concerns you, not by your anxious thoughts, not by your careful plans, but by My Spirit, for haven't I said, *"Not by might, nor by power, but by My Spirit."*[102]

The peace, the rest you seek, will come only as My Spirit is allowed to carry you at each moment through each circumstance, over each hurdle.

Am I faithful?

Can I be trusted to accomplish what needs to be done?

> You will not know nor see what really needs to be done unless you are empty. You won't really be free until you die to your plans, until you relinquish your perceived control, until you trust Me fully in everything.

Oh, but as you do, as you let go of your efforts to get anything done and begin to flow, oh, what peace, what rest will be yours!

Enter in.

Shared by Laura Wilcott

The Lovers' Path

It's not about you and what you can do or see or hear. I am working My work, so be at peace. Just enjoy Me. I AM your Great Reward. Remember, it's Me. It's not about where you're going. It's not about what you'll see. It's about Me. Let's just hold hands and enjoy the journey. Let's just walk together as two, taking a walk just to get to know each other.

Does it matter where they walk? Does it matter what they will see? Is it important how fast they travel or if any go along on the same path? Does it matter what they are wearing? Do two in love notice the scenery so much that they forget the one beside them? No, and yet My people want to take the bus! They are not interested in strolling hand in hand. They are too busy. They want the guided tour!

They peer out the window, catching a glimpse of Me as they pass by. The tour guides try to tell them about Me, yet they have not walked the path themselves. They haven't let Me whisper in their ear. They haven't gotten to know Me as those who walk beside Me.

They saw the path and the view and organized a tour—so much ambition, so much self, so much pride! They are so distorted in their thinking that they truly believe those who have chosen to walk instead, who are on the path instead of the seat beside them—are missing out!

They don't know that the road ahead is barricaded, that they will be stranded on the road—broken down. Some will choose to stay on the bus where they feel secure while the others will begin to stream out looking for the path, seeking to find what they missed, longing for Me, calling My Name.

Robbed of Precious Moments

Relax. Rest.

Be at peace.

Oh, My child, your many thoughts that bombard you from time to time, your many plans, cannot fill you as I can! They rob you of precious moments with Me. I'll fill your mind as no other can. I will direct your thoughts, but you must turn them to Me.

> You will never be able to walk in true peace until *your mind is stayed on Me.*[103]

Whatever is true, whatever is honorable, whatever is right, whatever is pure, whatever is lovely, whatever is commendable, if there is any excellence and if anything worthy of praise, think about these things.[104]

Oh, talk to Me about what bothers you. Let Me shed My Light on your circumstances.

Get My perspective.

Fill your mouth with those thoughts I give you of hope.

Just What the Enemy Wants

Oh, My child, I have everything you need.

I AM.

Draw from Me.

Let My words fill your mouth and your heart. Speak what *I* say, *not* the enemy. When you hear him speak in your ear, as your anxious thoughts surround you, don't voice it.

Don't give voice to those lies. Don't give him a foothold with your words. Don't give him a place.

For as you speak those words of discouragement and lies, you give the enemy just what he wants, but praise stills the avenger.

Turn your heart to Me quickly when circumstances seem difficult. Refuse, even cast down, those thoughts that bring contempt, division, strife, envy, lust, worry—anything that is not of My Spirit. For My *peace I leave with you, My peace I give to you; not as the world gives do I give to you. Let not your heart be troubled, neither let it be afraid.*[105]

Walk in My perfect peace.

Shared by Laura Wilcott

An Awesome Task at Hand

Make no mistake.

I am coming for My people.

I am breaking down the walls of separation and am coming for My people. Wake up! The dawn is here! I've sounded the alarm! I'm coming for My people.

Open the shudders! Throw open wide the door!

I'm coming for My people.

Raise high the banner! Gather the troops!

I'm coming for My people.

Say, "A new day, a new day is at hand, coming over the horizon, cresting even now!" See, as the people gather around My table, as they begin to enter in, as they are drawn up close to Me. Watch, as My Spirit rises within them, as their hearts are torn in two. Wait, and see this mighty work I am doing—this awesome task at hand!

[*Will you talk to me, Lord?*]

NOT ONLY WILL I TALK WITH YOU. I'LL POUR MY HEART OUT TO YOU. I AM READY TO REVEAL MY HEART TO YOU. IT IS NOT A QUESTION AS TO WHETHER I AM READY BUT YOU.

Stand Up! Say "No!"

Take control! Be observant, aware of each, and every, thought, and take control. Vanquish the offender! Do battle! Stand up and say, "Enough!" You no longer need to accept those inferior, even destructive, thoughts. No, you are free!

Stand up and proclaim your freedom! Stand your ground! Don't let those emotions that try to steal away your peace crash in around you. Say "No!"

> Be firm!
>
> Take charge!
>
> You're in control!

Emotions just reveal a deeper need, a course of correction. Look closer. Examine yourself. Why the rage, the anger, the hurt?

Is it pride that stands in your way?

This Isn't McDonalds!

Don't wait, My child. Don't wait for the tough times to enter into My bounty. For My table awaits. I have been waiting, longing for you to come sit with Me and dine. Oh, you run by My table on occasion to snatch a bite.

You grab and go. I barely have time to greet you as you whisk past Me. What's your hurry? Can't it wait? Whatever makes you rush? This isn't McDonalds! I don't have a drive-up window! If you want to get to know Me, you must sit down, you must listen, you must enjoy the meal.

"Chew slowly," I say. "Savor every bite. Take a drink. It's My wine made especially for you. Oh, feast to your heart's content! Oh, how I've waited for this day! Oh, what joy to have you finally join Me!"

You'll wonder why you waited so long. "What was it that was so important," you'll ask yourself, "that kept me away from my love, that stole my heart, that robbed my time? Oh, why didn't I heed His invitation? Why didn't I listen? Why didn't I come?"

You'll see that you were starving, famished, weak. Someone had been driving you around in circles. "What car was it?" you'll ask. Oh, My children are trapped inside of one car or another. Some find themselves inside religion, ambition, or activity.

The doors are locked. The driver won't slow down. You're getting tired of the ride. You're getting hungry. You consider jumping out, but he doesn't slow down. This car just doesn't stop! Everyone else doesn't seem to mind, but you're weary. Jump while you've got a chance!

No, it won't be easy. You'll be ridiculed, taunted, and teased. But when you get around that table of Mine, when you make it to your place, when you begin to feast in My Presence, when you drink of My wine, when you taste of My goodness, no one, I say, no one will be able to convince you that that ride is for you.

As they speed past My table, calling you to come and join, you'll wave them on, wondering when they'll get tired of the ride too, when they'll jump out and join you.

Fall on Me

Fall on Me.

I will carry you. I will make you stand. When the tempest rises around you,

fall on Me.

When your hopes get dashed,

fall on Me.

I AM your Strength and Support. I AM your Helper. Know Me. Commune with Me. Rely on Me. See My Love reach out to them and follow. See My hand of mercy, then speak. See Me. Oh, I AM there!

Acknowledge Me. Every moment, every moment, I AM there. Every trouble, every heartache, every frustration—I AM there. See Me. Look. Wait. I AM your very present help in times of trouble. I AM *all* that you need.

Acknowledge My Presence.

Wait for My Love.

Enter in.

Shared by Laura Wilcott

A Sweet Place

Oh, My child, it's not about you. I'm going to keep you. I'm going to hold you. I'm going to take you on this walk. I'm keeping your steps on the path. I'm leading the way. It's Me. It's not about you.

Just keep your eyes on Me, and you will move forward. Remember, it is I who is taking you on this journey. Don't start looking at yourself. Don't be deceived. Just press in.

You need to get so wrapped up in Me that nothing else interests you unless you invite Me along; nothing else can keep your attention unless I'm in it; nothing satisfies unless you are drinking from Me, from My well.

You'll be so consumed that the insults others throw at you will have no place to land. Like a glancing blow at first, then like a breeze as it blows past, then you'll find you can't hear them anymore. It will be as if they are speaking to someone else but not to you. I will muffle the enemy in your ears as if you were standing in another room far from the hurt, the pain, the anxiety. It will be far from you.

You won't care about *you* anymore, only about *them*. You won't need to be pampered, pleased, or comfortable. You won't need to be appreciated, thanked, or even remembered. No, I'm taking you to a place you've not been before, a sweet place, a sheltered place under My Wings to stay.

This time, I won't let go of you. This time, I won't let you run off. This is a secure place, not as you've known. This is the abiding place you've longed for. This is what your heart has been waiting for. I'm doing this thing. I'm drawing you in. I'm holding you close.

> I won't let you go.
>> It's been long enough. It's time.
>
> I'm taking your hand.
>> Just yield. I'll do the rest.

A Work Birthed in Them

Take a look over the horizon. What do you see? Take a look into the future. What do you observe?

> **Am I not your eyes, your ears, your voice? Am I not your very breath?**

Man tries to see without eyes, hear without ears, and speak without a tongue. Oh, man is nothing, has nothing, and can do nothing apart from the work that I have birthed in them!

> **They are deceived, enslaved, going nowhere, accomplishing nothing.**

Only with *My* eyes can they truly see reality. Only with *My* ears can they truly hear with revelation. Only *My* voice speaks to the glory of God. I am not here to trumpet man's accomplishments. No, My trumpet sounds out the glory of God. My trumpet heralds the victory I have wrought! Man sounds his own trumpet—one of pride, arrogance, and self. Whose trumpet will you hear? To whom will you give attention?

Created to Soar

Be steadfast, immovable, always abounding in the work of the Lord.[106]

RISE UP, I SAY! RISE UP!
        LET YOUR SPIRIT ARISE.

Don't be bowed down. Get your eyes off the path.

Look to the heavens. Set your gaze on Me. You were created to soar.

Let Me lift you up.

Let Me set you on high.

Sing! Rejoice! Shed the garments that have been weighing you down. Take on the garment of praise. Be clothed with adoration and thanksgiving. *Be dressed in righteousness. Be fitted with the helmet of salvation.*

Take up the Sword of the Spirit.[107] **Stand fast.**

For as you do, your spirit will arise out of the dust. Your countenance will begin to reflect My Glory. Your voice will begin to speak of My goodness, faithfulness, and Love. Your eyes will see My Beauty, your ears will hear a melody of peace, a symphony of praise, a shout of exultation!

As the Air They Breathe

Reach out! Reach out!

TAKE MY HAND.

FEEL MY TOUCH.

Open up! Yes, I'm drawing you in. Oh, yes, I'm making you aware of My Presence, more and more as you are able. Yes, I hide Myself. I must. Yet I begin to reveal Myself step by step to whom I wish.

I DRAW THEM IN.

I whisper in their ear.

I open their eyes, little by little.

They wait on Me. They learn to trust My voice. They learn to recognize My hand. They learn to listen. So many have a plan, a program, an agenda. They seek Me, they schedule Me according to a plan, then push Me out of their day. They relegate Me to a corner of their day, a moment of piety, a moment of sacrifice, yet I AM as the air they breathe.

I AM THEIR VERY BEING.

Oh, that they would wait on Me to draw them in, that they would be still and let Me envelop them! I would come if they would call. I would heal their blindness, but *they claim to see*.[108] I would cover their nakedness, I would fill their emptiness, I would hold their hand if they would just call out to Me.

Man thinks he has all the answers. He searches for more knowledge, yet wisdom eludes him. He cannot see his need. He seeks control but will have none.

Cherish the moments I draw you in.

Hovering over the Ground

Open up! Yes, open your wings! It is time to fly higher. You've been hovering over the ground, getting tired. Sure, you're off the ground. Yes, you've learned to flutter your wings, but what I have in store for you is so much better!

Take flight up to the higher heights.

I'll get you there.

I'll make a way.

I'm prepared to carry you to that place.

Rest. Rest for the journey ahead.

Rest, be still.

Have no worries. Have no concerns.

I will work everything out that I have called you to do. I will set you in your place, just as I have others, with ease in such a way as to bring glory to Me.

This Foolish Generation

You needn't worry about details. You needn't be concerned about others and what they think. I have set you on this path. I direct your feet. They cannot see the steps I tell you to take. They cannot hear the things I whisper in your ear.

THEY CANNOT KNOW MY PLAN.

Wake up to My realities. Don't sleep in this hour. *Be watchful. Be alert.* Only My Spirit knows My true workings in this hour. Man cannot see. Man cannot hear. Man is like a brute beast sniffing the wind, searching, hoping for his desires to be fulfilled.

> OH, THIS FOOLISH GENERATION SEES NOTHING BUT WHAT I HOLD UP IN FRONT OF ITS NOSE! IT HEARS NOTHING BUT WHAT I SHOUT! IT DOES NOTHING TO DRAW NEAR TO ME, THEIR SOURCE, BUT WHEN I SHAKE THEM!

Oh, callused and unfeeling are the many to My callings, My instructions, My ways!

In a Smoke-Filled Room

Take care. Be vigilant. Be attentive, for as the wind blows as a gale is approaching, so it is as My Spirit blows on the many.

> Don't stand by and miss My workings in this last hour.

> Oh, don't be blind to all that I am doing!

Oh yes, the time is short. For the work that I am working is but a breath away. As one breathes in the life-sustaining air, so it will be with many. It is as if they have been holding their breath in a smoke-filled room, looking for an exit sign. Those who have their eyes open, who see the sign, who have crawled to the door and stumbled out of the darkness. They take a deep breath.

The ones inside who will not stoop see nothing but black darkness and terror. They will take a breath, but not the one they want. The exit sign will be obscured from their view until they bend their knee.

Listen carefully. According to a predetermined plan are the events that have been set in motion. Look not for signs in the natural, even though you will see gusts from the things I am doing.

> **CAN'T YOU SEE THE PLAN I HAVE INVOLVES THE HEARTS OF MEN, NOT THEIR HANDS.**

Man judges all things by the exterior. He sizes up a situation with his natural eyes; he can see no further. He is so limited.

Shared by Laura Wilcott

My precious faithful ones look far beyond into My realm. Their vision is vast. They perceive much in the Spirit. They aren't interested in what interests others.

Staggering Under the Weight

It's time for the weary to come home. It's time for the weary to find rest, and rest is what they will find—a peaceful rest, free from concern and worry, free from shoulds and should-haves, *a rest built upon a promise.*[109]

> Oh, yes, they will find their way to that safe place. They will be escorted by My Spirit, brought on My sure and steady Wings, carried in My arms to that place I have for them.

Yes, they will see it and rejoice in that day, for the load they were carrying, the burden on their back was too much for them to bear. They've been staggering under the weight of it for too long—oppressed, enslaved, and bound up by all that man tried to put on them, all that man thinks I require.

Oh, if only they could see My abundant mercy, My infinite grace, My steadfast Love, they wouldn't heap these burdens upon themselves and others! They would run free, as a child runs in a meadow, and shout to all who would hear, "I'm free! I'm free! I'm free!"

Yes, when I set a man free, no one can carry him back to that place of bondage, to those chains of fear, to that consuming darkness. He is free to enjoy My Love, My grace, My goodness—My rest.

Take a Deep Breath

Oh yes, it will be frustrating and even agonizing at times to those who can't seem to be freed from their sin. As I have said, they will long for relief and won't find it, not until I draw them, not until I call their name, not until I set them free *then they will be free indeed.*[110] No, they won't have to struggle any longer. No, they won't have to contend with the flesh, for the freedom that I offer is absolute, perfect, complete.

Oh, My child, lean on Me more.

Call out to Me more. Listen to Me even more, and yes, I will refresh you more. I will restore you even more. I will replenish you. Just drink! Drink to your heart's delight.

Let this be a time of renewal, a refreshing time to rejuvenate your spirit. Oh, I have so much more in store for you, so much waiting at your feet! You just need to breathe in. You're tired. You've wandered around too long. You're thirsty. You're famished.

Oh, My child, your journey has ended. Your wandering is over. You've come to that resting place. You've arrived at that safe haven.

Just sit down and take a deep breath.

I'll do the rest.

I'll breathe into your spirit.

On the Very Edge

Higher and higher, deeper and deeper, farther and farther will the journey be as you cast off your old thinking, your old ideas, your old plans, and breathe in My Life. For the breath of God sustains you.

Breathe in deeply.

Oh, My child, let the times and the seasons not pass you by as a river runs its course, whether the one on the bank jumps in or not. You have seen so much. You have heard in your ear wonders, and yet you hesitate to step in and be consumed. Jump in! I'll carry you. Don't let all that I'm doing pass you by. Oh, don't hold back!

Be released! Be free!

Take a deep breath. I will fill you. You are on the very edge.

Let go!

You won't be disappointed. *Let go of that sin that so easily weighs you down.*[111]

Be free!

It's right before you. I've laid it at your feet.

Where Fear Is but a Memory

Oh, take command of those feelings, those thoughts! Take charge! Don't allow yourself to be bound up any longer!

You are free!

I've purchased your freedom! I've made it available!

Step into what I've already provided! Don't miss out on what is already yours! For as you do, as you break loose of those chains, as you begin to run free, I will pick you up and carry you to new heights in the Spirit, places you've never been but only dreamed of.

> ## I'll take you to a place where fear is but a memory, where anxiety and worry don't exist, where anger and rage can't abide.

I'll take you to that place. I'll carry you through that door. Just open up your heart. Take Me in. Be consumed. As a rushing wind, I'll come in if you'll open the door wide.

> Only rest. Don't strive to be.
>
> Only wait. Don't jump ahead.
>
> Only stand.

The Benefit of Doing It My Way

Yes, I have planted you. And yes, you will sprout and grow and produce much fruit, but even a seed takes time to come forth.

There is a time of being hidden,

a time of being still,

a time of waiting,

yes, even a time of dying.

No, it won't take long, but it is necessary. All your waiting, all your watching, all your listening will be richly rewarded. The benefit of doing it My way you will see so clearly.

So be vigilant as My faithful soldier.

As a Picture Painted on a Wall

Stand watch.

Wait for instruction.

Be patient.

For don't you believe that Elijah, when he mocked the prophets of Baal, knew and had seen the victory, knew and had seen the outcome, knew and had seen their demise? Oh yes, he saw! As a picture painted on a wall that comes to life, he saw what others could not see. He saw what others would refuse to believe. He saw, and when he saw, he believed! When he saw, he received!

So look! Look in the Spirit.

Look carefully.

Look closely.

Wait and you too will see!

For I am doing a work and long to reveal it to My children. I long for My mature sons and daughters to open their eyes and look at what I'm doing. For when they stop all and look into My realm, they will see what their mind will scream cannot be true but what their heart rejoices to see.

So don't give up. Keep waiting, keep watching, keep listening, for in it is much reward!

What a Mess!

Oh, yes, you've seen what you're made of and don't like it. You've walked in defeat, yes, even defiance at times, and can't seem to get your bearings. You've wandered around in the wilderness seeking a drink. You've called out My Name yet tried to pave a way without Me.

When will it end? When will you give up? When will you just sit down and say, "I've had enough!" When will you finally let go? You'll not find anything that satisfies like I do. No amount of control can bring joy.

Only when you allow Me to be God, only when you give Me your children's hearts, only when you acknowledge that I'm Lord will you see victory. When they don't cooperate, say, "Lord?" and wait on Me. Yes, truly look to Me for your answer. You don't have it, and they know it.

You can't see the road—only Me. You can't and don't know how to deal with them—only Me. You don't know what will prick their heart, what will stir their spirit like I do. You only wander around in darkness, causing pain. What a mess you can make apart from Me!

["*Where do I go from here?*" *I asked.*]

Give them to Me. They are not yours. They never were. Let Me raise them, nurture them, love them. I know how. Just yield. Throw your hands up and yield. Yield to My workings. Yield to My ways. Be no longer driven but led.

Oh, take of Me and give out to the children. Drink of Me and water their souls. Eat of Me and feed them. Yes, be to them what I've called you to be—a refreshing fountain of Life.

A Deep Reservoir

[I cried, Oh, Lord, I just want to enjoy You!]

He answered, Oh, yes, you will! Yes, indeed, you will! You needn't worry, little one; you needn't fret, for I will see to it that your reservoir is deep and wide and full to overflowing. Richly blessed, yes, abundantly supplied, reinforced on every side, undergirded with strength, endowed with wisdom, controlled by Love—this is how you will walk in My Kingdom; this is how you will rule at My command.

No more will you say, "Help me, Lord!" For you will know I am your very present help in times of trouble.[112] You'll say, "Thank You, Lord!" for who I AM in you. I will rise up inside of you. I will cause you to walk, to run, to fly, to soar over all you've been under before.

You'll take your stand.

You will know Me and My Love.

You will know Me and the fellowship of My sufferings.[113]

You will know My Power, My Might, My Glory.

Oh, rich blessing, rich indeed will your reward be as you follow Me, turning not to the right nor to the left, waiting, watching, and resting.

Dear to Me

Dear sweet child, that's what you are to Me, dear to My heart.

[*But why, Lord?*]

I've told you time and again that those of Mine who throw themselves onto Me and My grace, who cast themselves without reserve onto My mercy, who wait upon My hand are precious—dear to Me. I AM their hope, their joy, their satisfaction.

OH, THAT ALL MY CHILDREN WOULD TRUST ME AND WAIT ON ME TO RISE WITHIN THEM!

Instead, they run ahead. They don't understand that the very act of waiting, trusting, resting is so needful, so absolutely necessary. They stand in the way every time they try to help Me.

What a mess My children get into every time they jump when I begin to stir them! Pride propels them. Ego drives them on. If only they would surrender, if only they would yield, if only they would bow!

I wait patiently for them to get tired of their pursuits, their ambitions, yes, their pride until they see that nothing they do brings results, nothing, absolutely *nothing, they can do brings victory.*[114]

Make Up Your Mind

Settle it once and for all in your spirit. Make up your mind who's in charge. Don't be double-minded. If it's Me, then move over. Take charge of those thoughts that say otherwise.

> Resist those lies!
>
> Stand firm!

You've seen how to do it. You know when you're tempted.

> Walk away!

Run to Me! You're tired of playing God but not nearly as tired as I am of your games. Cease your efforts to control anyone.

> Stop your manipulation.
>
> Quit trying to run things.
>
> It's time.

Yes, you'll stand in the way. Yes, you'll impede the process if you don't step out of the way. Drop your agenda to change people, even your children. That's *My* job. That's *My* specialty. When I rise up inside of a precious one, others will know it is Me. You won't have to do a thing, so stop your interference into My business.

Shared by Laura Wilcott

Quit Playing God!

Quit playing God!

I already told you I didn't need any help. Do you really believe you can change a heart? Do you think for a moment you can mold a character? Do you honestly believe you can instill wisdom into another without My help?

No, you just get in the way when you nag. If only you would trust Me. If only you would stand back and watch Me work. If only you would let go and see My Glory.

> When will you enter in? When will you cast all of yourself over onto Me? When will you wait upon Me to carry you, hold you, keep you?

I've been waiting, watching for you to abandon yourself to Me, to run into My arms without reserve, without restraint, without hesitation.

Come, oh come.

I'm here.

I LOVE YOU.

DON'T EVER DOUBT MY LOVE.

My Bride

Oh, take My hand. You've waited long enough. You've tarried. You've sought Me but not earnestly. Oh, you've waited, but just for a moment. Oh, there is so much more!

Take My hand. Don't put Me off any longer. Don't weary Me. Don't grieve My Spirit. For I'm waiting for you. I'm longing for you. I'm weary of waiting.

Oh, it's My arms that ache. Now you know, now you've had a glimpse, just a taste of what My heart feels. Oh, don't keep Me waiting. Don't weary Me any longer. Don't stay away. Come closer—so very much closer. I'm here waiting, watching, longing, hoping, yearning for your love, for you to finally press in and take hold of Me. My arms are aching. Don't pass Me by.

I've been here all along. My children just can't see; they don't want to believe; they can't fathom that My heart aches for them, that they are all I think about, all I care about, all I long for—My bride[115]—spotted as she is, disheveled, wrinkled, distracted, disinterested, looking everywhere but to Me, searching, hoping, longing for everything but Me. But then, as I begin to open her eyes, as I begin to call her name, as I begin to woo her to Me, as I show her she's washed, as I touch her, as I hold her, as I caress her lovingly and with tender care—she'll come.

Oh, she won't stay away. She won't resist.

Oh, it's time.

Much More to Come

Oh, My child, you've come a long way, and yet there is much more to come. You've seen many things, yet so many things are left unseen.

> You've heard,
>
> you've tasted,
>
> you've touched,
>
> and yet not as you will.[116]

Be assured, yes, be very sure that nothing of what you have received has come by your will, nor has it come by your works, nor has it come by your wisdom. No, My Word has come to you by *My* will, *My* wisdom, *My* works.

Open up even more.

Yes, you know who you are. You know what you've seen. You know what you've heard. And yet, you don't know as you will know, you don't see as you will see, you don't hear as you will hear.

> ### Oh, I couldn't tell you now, nor could I show you what is in store in the coming days, for your mind has not been renewed enough.

Shout It If You Have To

You must die to your old thinking of who you were.

> You must crucify those thoughts that say
>
> you can't,
>
> you aren't,
>
> you won't.
>
> No, that is of the enemy.

He wants to keep you down when I *will* to raise you up. He wants to keep you quiet when I say, "Speak!"

Oh, that cunning, crafty one uses any means possible to keep you from what I have in store for you, yet he will not succeed. For you have seen on the other side and know it is glorious!

> No, he won't have his way,
>
> not today nor tomorrow.

Just start saying what I say. Speak it aloud! Shout it if you have to! But keep My Word ever before you. Stay focused only on Me, and you will progress forward. Yes, you will come into all I have prepared for you and reap the reward—and yes, there will be a reward—a great reward!

Right at Your Feet

Rest. Rest your mind.

Be still.

Be quiet.

Take moments, as I draw you in, to rest, to rest your weary soul.

Be at peace.

It's time. It's time for your striving to come to an end.

Haven't I shown you so many times how your anxious efforts lead nowhere? Your anxieties weigh heavy on you when you cease to rest when you fail to listen. Now is the time, the very day you've been waiting for. It's at the door, all you've hoped for, everything you've dreamed of. It's right here, at your feet. I'll take that heart of yours and mold it. I'll take your will, too. That stubborn pride has to go—none of it can stay!

Oh, how pride gets in the way! It's a disease that infects the soul. Be free! Say, "No!" Don't let it have a place any longer. *You need to run, no longer weighed down.*[117] You need to soar, no longer under this burden. Throw it off!

It's time!

Prevailing to the Point of Peace

Be prepared. Look up. Take action when you see Me move. The next step is one of prevailing, yes, prevailing to the point of peace, peace when you walk about, peace when you stand, and even peace when you sleep.

It won't be as you've known before. This place I'm bringing you to is a resting place. I know you've sought rest, and now you have it! You've sought relief, and now it's yours! Oh, be exceedingly glad, for today is your day of victory! It's finally come!

Reach out. Grasp My hand, My strong arm. Don't be hesitant. Don't shy away. Don't step back.

> **Reach out. Grab a hold of Me,
> for I AM what you need.**

Don't be deceived into thinking that what you need is out there somewhere. Search no longer. Look not to your right nor to your left. Keep your eyes fixed on Me.

> WHO AM I? WHAT DO I HOLD IN MY HAND? AM I NOT THE ONE WHO FILLS ALL IN ALL? AM I NOT YOUR FAITHFUL FRIEND? AM I NOT YOUR FATHER WHO CARES FOR YOU, *WHO HOLDS YOUR HAND?*[118] CAN I NOT BRING ABOUT ALL THAT I'VE PROMISED? WILL I NOT DO IT?

Running Around on Empty

Oh, get to know Me. Don't stay at arm's length.

Come closer.

Let Me breathe on you. Let Me fill you with who I AM.

Let Me hold you close.

Oh, My child, there is so much more! You've been running around on empty. Fill up from My well. Don't try to give out from an empty cup.

Fill up.

Drink of Me.

Consume Me.

Be refreshed from My fountain.

Oh, My people hear of a well nearby and immediately begin to gather cups to share with others, yet they never come near enough to get a drink themselves. Throw down your cup and step in! When they see you drenched with Me, they will not be satisfied with a cup any longer. They will jump in and join you.

Shared by Laura Wilcott

Give Out from the Well

Oh, take My hand as you lead the children. Don't go it alone. I have the wisdom you need. Draw from My vast supply.

Stop, wait, listen.

Don't be quick in your dealings with the children. Step back and get My perspective before you act.

> Oh, what you want from Me, loving kindness and mercy, give to your children!

Give out from the well. Draw from Me. I'm a deep reservoir. Don't pass Me by.

> Oh, that you would see the treasure you hold in your hand! Oh, that you would realize they are My treasure!

Treat them with loving care. Treat them with mercy. I'll show you how. Love your children as yourself.

Stop reaching for change, but delight in Me. The change will come, not as you expect, for you expect instant results. I work through the trials. No, you cannot produce the change, so stop trying. Let Me do it.

Shared by Laura Wilcott

Love Them Gently

Don't look at the children in judgment.

Love them.

Don't be so harsh.

Be gentle.

Mold them gently. Take them carefully in your hand.

Don't break their spirit. Don't be quick in your dealings with them. Don't be so stern. Love them gently. Deal with them in love.

Be gracious, gentle, and kind. I will enable you to walk this way.

Yield to Me.

Let Me help you. Let Me be your teacher.

Lean on Me.

Consult Me.

Follow Me.

I long to lead you.

The Wrong Frequency

Notice, take note, I am doing a new thing. I am causing the winds of change to blow in from the east. I am making it blow. It will be a gale. "The storm is upon us!" they will cry. Gale force winds! Batten down the hatches. Anchor your soul. Cast not away from you, your confidence. Guard the treasure inside. Be to them a beacon of Light. Be to them a lighthouse on the Rock. As their vessels crash around you, some will see it, some will come, some will maneuver past the dangers past the treacherous waters to a safe harbor—to a place of refuge.

Be watchful. Be alert. Be ready, for it has come upon you, even now! I will blind the eyes, some of them, to that safe harbor. I will cause their waters to be rough. I will cause the sea to swallow them—their vessels to go down, their life rafts, their hope, will seem to dash upon rocks. Oh, what destruction they will see! Oh, what desolation that will come their way! But you—stand. Be immovable. Resound My praises! Resound My high praises in your mouth, for the day is upon them!

Yes, it will come, and those not heeding the warnings, not watching the signs, will be dashed upon the Rock with no one to rescue, with no one to hear their cries. The waves will pound around you. The sea will roar. The vessels will crash at your side.

No, unless one has learned to take shelter under My Wings, to abide in that safe place,[119] they will be distraught and in anguish at what they see and hear. No, you are not to look with those eyes nor hear with those ears. Be watchful! Be alert! Stay awake on this your watch! Sound the alarm on this holy mountain!

Shared by Laura Wilcott

Stoke the fire! Tend the embers! Fan the flames! Be to them what I've called you to be. May My faithful ones burn brightly. May their lamp not go out. May the shining Light go out from them to those around.

Spread abroad the Light of My Countenance! Spread abroad the Light I've given you! They will see it. They will come. My Light draws many. They can't stay away. They are drawn in. Wait and see.

> [*In my mind's eye, I pictured a man at the helm of a small ship on a stormy sea. He was wearing headphones so he could hear the radio transmission. I knew the voice coming over the wire was the Holy Spirit's, giving precise direction to the safe harbor.*]

Those tuned in will hear it—those on the right frequency. Many will be tuned in, all ears, to the wrong frequency. Man has said, "This is it. This is the frequency," but in times of trouble, they will hear static. They were persuaded. They were deceived.

Those who have been listening will hear their instructions very clearly. They are like those with headphones, who have purchased them to block out the noise, to hear their instructions clearly, so when the storm is upon them, they do not hear the crashing of the waves or the gale force winds, just that peaceful voice leading them home.

As the Waves Begin to Rise

It is necessary for you to endure hardship as a good soldier, not to break ranks, not to retreat, not to give in. For the things I desire to do through you require a patient endurance, a steady calm throughout the course of the storm, not yielding to the wind or being buffeted by the waves. You must stand steady, firm, immovable as the waves crash against the vessel.

This will be so, yet only as you yield yourself as the waves begin to rise. Don't look at the wind and the waves as Peter did. Don't set your eyes on what doesn't last.

> For I AM He who holds the winds of life in My hands. I AM He who calms the storm or makes it arise. I AM He who speaks, and it is so.

Look to Me, for I desire to set you above the storms of life, to have you walk above the raging waters, but you must keep your eyes fixed on Me at all times.

I will hold your hand. Let Me be the center of your soul.

Let Me hold you closer. *Come closer.*

Every moment, lean on Me.

Carry Them If You Have To

Reach out as I begin to fill you. Take the hand of the one beside you and show him the way. Reach out to those around you. Carry them if you have to. Hold them close. Listen to their cries.

Open up to their longings, their needs.

Don't be deaf to the voice of their cry, for they are as you were—lost and alone. They stumble in the dark, looking for some light, a ray of hope, a voice of cheer.

Reach out to those around you!

Reach out.

Let Me show you My heart of love. Let Me fill you up. Step out of the way. Move over. I have more than enough concern for your brothers and sisters. I have more than enough love for the world. You don't need to look for it or search in any way.

My Love is all around you, in you.

Just rest, just wait, you'll see. I'll perform this work in you. I'll rise up from within.

That Door of Love

Oh, gently, will I lead you. Gently, will I hold your hand and take you through that door of love. You won't have to struggle to get there. It won't be an effort. Just enter in.

Seek peace and pursue it.

Call to mind My tender mercies.

OH, HOW I LONG FOR YOU TO STEP INTO MY TENDER MERCIES.

Just jump. Abandon yourself. Oh, it's not enough to talk of My love. No, you must respond to My Love. I long to love through you. I long to see you mature.

Stay hidden in the Secret Place. Stay sheltered in *the Rock*.[120] Abide. Abide. Abide. That is the key.

OH, I AM LOVE.

KNOW ME.

COMMUNE WITH ME.

REST.

Shared by Laura Wilcott

It Tastes No Different

Watch every word that I have spoken in your ear. Diligently observe My promises, for not one word has been released without a purpose. Each and every one carries a message for someone.

Oh, you are appointed, you are placed, you are established to carry My Word to those I've chosen. You will take of mine and give out to the brethren. You will shed abroad those treasures entrusted to you. Look and see what I have placed before you. Call to mind what I have spoken in your ear. Is there anything you did, is there anything you said, is there anything you prayed to cause My hand to bring such a thing to pass?

No! Only by My grace, only by My divine purposes have I caused your life to be as a waterfall.

The river has no power of its own to continue on a smooth course

if a

cliff

is

placed

before it.

The water in a river is the same as the water of the waterfall. The steeper and more treacherous the course, the more they gaze, yet if you take the water and put it in a glass, it tastes no different. *Don't look as man looks. See with My eyes.*

Beyond What You Can Imagine

Don't get caught up in the details of life, in the mundane aspects of each day. No! For as I lead you step by step, you will venture into a higher realm than you have seen, higher than you can grasp at this moment—beyond what you can imagine. So enter in. *Press in.*

> Jump in to My river. Oh, jump in!

Don't keep to yourself. Don't settle into fear. Don't accept an inferior path, for you must rise above all that. Don't be as those not ready to enter in. Don't be stagnate.

> Be washed with pure water.
> > Be filled from My streams of water.
> > > Be overflowing from My cup.

For everything is in due time. You will enter into that realm I have for you, so rest. Take it easy.

> Be at peace in My Presence.
> > Be enveloped in My Love.

I want to plant you beside the still waters. I want to refresh you. If you will just wade into My waters, I'll teach you how to swim.

I AM *ALL* YOU NEED.

Clouded by Wants

Oh, won't you learn? Why won't you learn of Me? You look here. You search there. But you won't find what I, and only I, can give you. Don't chase after things that don't last. Don't set your eyes on what's fleeting. I will provide those things you need.

> Keep your eyes on My Kingdom.
>
> Fix your gaze on Me.
>
> **For I speak, and it is done. I call forth every provision.**

So many of My children go astray and don't seek the Author of life because their vision is clouded by wants. You will rise above this earthly realm. You have set your sights on My Kingdom, and you will be fulfilled.

Oh, that My children would want Me!

The Higher Realm

Answer those who would question My voice. Say to them what I speak in your ear. Don't be timid, for I *will* to grow them up. I *will* to see them mature. I *will* for My children to walk in My Kingdom, free from entanglements, exercising the authority I have given them.

> Know this Power
> that comes from authority.
>
> Know this awesome power at your disposal.
>
> It is in your hand. It is on your tongue.

I will to reveal My Power to you. I will to make it known to you. Yes, you will see mighty works in the days ahead. You will witness the miraculous, so don't be astonished when you see My Kingdom unfold before your eyes. This is the realm in which I wish for you to walk. This is the higher realm.

Keep your eyes opened, your ears attentive, for it will get clearer and clearer. All that I desire for your life has already been preordained. It has already been established, set in place for you to walk.

No matter what comes, no matter what others may say, I want you to realize that My Kingdom is not perceived by natural means. Those who remain in the natural realm, in the soul realm, cannot sense the workings of My Spirit in the Kingdom realm. You must live in this realm.

No Longer Speaking for the Enemy!

I cause the crooked places to be straight as I will in your life. Hearken unto Me. Let your voice be heard, no longer speaking for the enemy. Let your tongue no longer be an instrument for his devices. You will hold your tongue! I will see to it!

> You are to be an *instrument of righteousness*,[121] one of praise to our God.
>
> You are to display His Glory!

You are to be a *vessel of mercy*[122] poured out for the many. This will begin with your mouth. The unconditional love you have longed for will begin in your mouth by your lips. Your lips will bring healing and restoration. They will nurture and admonish in love. They will not speak on their own initiative. They will be muzzled to deception. You will see the divisiveness of the devil through words. These words will no longer hold you in bondage.

> You are free!

You are set free from the enemy's hold on your tongue!

> Rejoice! Rejoice this day!

For He has caused a great victory to be wrought!

> You will see it come to pass!

Shared by Laura Wilcott

The Real Happenings

Oh, the time is short. We have but a moment left, a blink of the eye. For the things I have spoken in your ear are surely most definitely coming to pass even before your very eyes. No, the naked natural eye can only see what man sees. How many times do I have to tell you to stop looking with these eyes? They will leave you lacking in knowledge.

You must turn your attention to the realm of the Spirit—My realm. Live in it, move, walk, rest in it, for the real happenings are all around you. Perceive them! Know My work!

Don't be blind in this last hour.

Stay focused.

Be alert!

Be watchful as I said.

Yes, I will make a way for *those plans I have for you*.[123] I will bring them to pass. Don't strive. *Follow Me.* Don't get distracted. Keep your eyes fixed, focused, open!

Next will come a *threshing among the wheat*.[124] Watch, see it even now. Be observant in the Spirit. Be attentive to what's going on around you, in you. I'm doing this very work in multitudes, My child, multitudes. You are not alone. Oh, no!

Of Nothing Are You More Sure

I have called you to be a voice of My Spirit. You must obey. You must say the things I have for you to say. I'll lead you. You are not alone.

You must follow the leading of the Spirit, for a time is coming when men will long to hear words of encouragement. Make sure when I'm speaking that you don't jump ahead. I will tell you of things to come but that have not yet been ordained to be revealed to others.

>Rely on My voice to lead you.
>
>>Rely on My Spirit to direct your steps.

They will cause you to know the right path. They will cause you to speak an apt word in due season.

>Trust in My leading.

Don't look to man for verification of what I say. *You know My voice!*[125] I don't need man's approval.

>You can hear!

Don't ask man, any longer, his opinion when you've heard Me speak, when you know it's Me.

A Path Swept Clean

Like dew of a morning, like rain at noon, and like an evening shower will My Word come to you—refreshing, reviving, restoring—yet increasing, increasing to the point that nothing in the natural is clearer. Of nothing are you more sure than what you've heard and what you've seen.

Clearly will you see My Kingdom. Clearly will you walk through the door laid out for you. *You will not stumble from what others stumble.*[126] Your path will be clear like a path swept clean. Your way will not be hindered. I will cause you to walk securely without fear of falling, without fear of losing your way.

Now, take what I've given you thus far and hold on to it. Keep it with you when you walk by the way. Store it in your heart for the day to come. You will see all these things come to pass, just as I've said. See to it that you do not take lightly the instruction of the Lord, for nothing disclosed is without purpose, nothing revealed is without a plan.

I cause you to see, I cause you to hear for a reason.

YOU ARE TO BE A CHANNEL, A RIVER OF LIFE TO MANY.

Vast, Explosive, Dynamic

Now is the time you will see, and you will taste, and you will touch things of which you have just imagined. For I am doing a new thing! *I am setting before you an opened door that no one can shut.*[127] Things you have seen before will seem as nothing compared to that which I am about to show you. For My Kingdom realm is vast, explosive, dynamic, beyond what you could even begin to comprehend. But you will comprehend it in part. You will begin to see with a new vision, My vision.

Oh, all that I have for you in the coming days will consume you to the point there is no longer you—but Me. What you have experienced, what you have seen, what you have perceived thus far is but a drop in a bucket compared to what I have planned for you, so don't think we have time to waste. Don't think for a moment that we can or will drag out feet, for I will not!

I am busy about what I am doing in My faithful ones. I am tending to My business diligently, and so you must also. You must be diligent. Your diligence has been based in the past on your carnal desires, not on My desires, but this will all change.

As a man keeps watch over a city at night, so, I keep watch over you.

Don't trouble yourself with what I haven't introduced to you thus far. Don't be concerned with matters beyond you. *Just seek Me. Rest in Me. Enjoy Me.*

For I will bring you to the place you need to be. I can straighten out your thinking. Don't think this is difficult for Me, for it is not! *Relax! Be free! Rest!*

[*In my mind's eye, I saw a man on a horse. He had a purple robe with a brilliant collar made of gold. He wore on his side a sword in a sheath. The sheath was gold with large, majestic gemstones, rectangular and of different colors, inlaid down its length. He drew his sword, held it high, and with a loud voice declared,*

"CHILD OF GOD, DAUGHTER OF THE MOST HIGH, BEGIN TO REIGN!"]

Stand in the Gap!

There is so much more! You're not to instruct your husband anymore. I've called you to pray for him, to help him, to minister to him—not to instruct him. You are to pray! You've been appointed. Take this seriously. You've been called. He can't hear Me when you're talking. He can't see Me when you are standing in the way. He can't get to know Me when you are distracting him. Quit interfering.

Be My ambassador only as I speak. What kind of ambassador speaks out of turn. They can only speak with authority when they've been commissioned to speak. You are commissioned to pray! Stand in the gap! Run to the altar! Hold up your husband *before the throne of grace.*[128]

Don't weary Me with this petty, inferior conversation—I'm tired of it. Be what I've called you to be. Rise up and stand. Now is the time for you to surrender your tongue, to be master over your words. I will hold your tongue. I will help you as before. I will enable you—just yield.

Pray every time. Pray! Pray when you haven't been given anything to say. Pray! Pray the answer. Pray and see Me act on his behalf! Pray and see Me move! Pray and see My Glory!

What a glorious day when my children will surrender their will to Mine! What a glorious moment when they finally give their tongues to Me and let Me have My way! Then they will truly be a vessel of glory, *a vessel of honor, a vessel that I can use, fit for every good work.*[129] Oh, you won't regret it! Just yield.

Shared by Laura Wilcott

More than Enough

Abundantly supplied for each and every endeavor, adequately equipped for every service, reinforced on every side are My children as they walk into My provision, as they yield to My Spirit, as they follow My lead.

> What general sends his troops into action without adequate provision? What king's entourage lacks the proper supplies?

Not only am I well able to meet every need, I am standing with arms outstretched, waiting for My children to see their inheritance to see the reserve stored up for them as they rise up in obedience to My commands.

I am not an impotent God.

I don't need bake sales, fundraisers, or gimmicks for My work to proceed. I don't need a cleverly devised marketing campaign for My Kingdom to reign. My purposes will be fulfilled without any superstar's endorsement or corporate sponsorship.

I AM all in all.

My children need only to wait on Me when they have a need and watch expectantly. They need only to trust. As they do, My hand will bring their provision.

That Entrance of Peace

Rest. Take it easy. I'll be your abiding place. Remember I AM your Shelter from the storm.

> Just turn to Me.
>
> Rest on Me.
>
> Call out to Me.

Take each moment as an opportunity to press into Me, not heeding the voices that try to stir you up, not giving into the lies that try to bring you down. *Just stand, and when you've done all—stand.*[130]

> Focus on Me in each trial! Attend to My voice of instruction. Turn to Me quickly. Inquire of Me.

I'll help you through. I'll hold your hand.

> I'll walk beside you into that door of love through that entrance of peace.

Step in! Throw off those old clothes! Throw off that baggage, those rags! Step in, I say! Step into that abiding place—that place of rest.

> It's home.

Shared by Laura Wilcott

You've been wandering around, seeking rest from the emotions of each moment, seeking refuge. Enter in! I AM that Refuge, that Abiding Place.

THROW OFF THOSE GRAVE CLOTHES!

Don't stay out in the cold, where the icy winds blow. Don't hold on in stubborn pride to your rights, for you have none. No. *You've been crucified with Christ, nevertheless you live.*[131]

> *Don't walk around as a dead man with grave clothes around you. Be free! I've set you free! I've called you forth! I've shouted your name!*[132]
>
> BE FREE!

Walk in that freedom I've purchased! *Stand in that grace I've supplied!*

> *Reign in My Kingdom!*
>
> *Reign through My Power, by My Spirit!*[133]
>
> **Yes, I say, today is a day to reign!**

Get up! Stand to your feet! No more bowing down. No more wandering around in defeat. You will reign! Today, as you mount up by My Spirit on My Wings, you will shake off the dust. You will take flight. You will begin to soar.

Yes, leaving behind those weights, those entanglements, those burdens looking to a better place, you will soar above all that you were bound by, all that has been weighing you down.

"No more!" you'll say. "No more!" For the enemy has lost hold of one. He has lost hold and cannot have you again. So rejoice! I say, rejoice!

A Gathering of the Camps

Predestined for My glory are many in the coming days, marked out to receive an abundance of rain. Appointed for the task, for the privilege of setting the Body in its place are the few who consider My ways, who give heed to My voice.

> They run on the wall. They burst through the defenses. Their mouths give flight to the enemy and have him scurrying on his way. They command, and it is so.

They call down judgment along the path on those who set their face to do evil in My sight, on those who seek their own profit and glory.

Keep your eyes on My path. Watch your steps.

> **Go forward in the Spirit.**
>
> **Don't drag your feet.**

Oh, My message is for today, for it is well spent! Tomorrow is close at hand and brings a gathering of the camps into one—one organism beating in unison, one fire-breathing entity that will *carry out My orders on the nations.*[134]

Eating Hotdogs in the Stands

Take your place. Step up to the plate. Don't watch the stands, for those in the stands will suffer loss. They will be filled with the fruit of their ways.

> Stay in the game.

> I will coach you.

You will receive your instructions as the coach at first base instructs the runner as he watches what goes on on the field. He has the runners running in unison. They receive their commands.

> They are off!

> They don't look back.

Check your bat, your shoes, your helmet. You are not eating hotdogs in the stands. You are not concerned whether you have coke or chips. You just keep your eyes on the man at the base. Watch him closely. For we have the ball. We have control of the game. We've set them in their place. We've instructed them in their position, prepared them, equipped them.

> Let's play the game!

Oh, those in the stands don't know what they are missing. They think it's a spectators' sport! Concessions are on their mind. They'll root you on, not knowing they are on the roster, too, not perceiving they are up to bat next.

Shared by Laura Wilcott

Stumbling Around in the Dark

Cast away any doubt you have of My goodness.

You will see, in the coming days, many who follow their own way, who stumble in the dark, who seek to establish their own righteousness and have not known Mine. You will see them as if they stumbled onto a bright path leading in another direction.

They will be in awe of My grace, My goodness, My mercy!

Oh, what joy will be theirs!

Oh, what rejoicing in that day!

[I could see people stumbling out of a thick underbrush that had been obscuring their vision. They stumbled out—confused, disoriented—onto a clear, bright path leading at right angles from where they had been heading. They didn't know it was there and looked surprised to be standing on the path.]

Oh, it's time for you to open your eyes! See what I'm doing! Look! Watch! You won't be blind. You won't stumble around in the dark anymore. Now is the time to look into the spirit realm and perceive. Don't stay in the dark. You don't need to. The lighted path is opened up before you, right at your feet.

> I AM LIGHT.[135] I AM THAT ILLUMINATION YOU'VE SOUGHT.

See yourself in My realm, walking in My Love, abiding in My Presence, reigning at My hand.

In your times with Me relax, for I will teach you the way. I will do the work. Rest in Me. I will cause the growth. Just enjoy Me.

Speak That Precious Message

Oh, slow of heart are My people to believe My words given for them! They seek pleasure and comfort, yet they are tormented in soul.

> **Hold up a standard. Raise it up.**

Call unto My people to stand, rise, and walk.

> **I'll show you each step.**

> **I'll direct you in the way.**

My desire is to counsel you, step by step, into what I have for you to say. My desire is to speak through you words of Life, words of hope, words birthed for the moment.

Don't Shut Up That River

You are to speak as My Spirit speaks.

You are to flow as My Spirit flows through you.

Yes, you will share My words with the brethren, but only as your brethren open up to Me for fresh *manna*. Do not think for a moment that I cannot instruct My children in any fashion I see fit.

I *will* to speak through you.

I *will* to make My words known, but only as I speak. Testify to your brethren of My mighty Power.

BEGIN TO WALK THAT WALK I HAVE FOR YOU. BEGIN TO ABIDE IN MY PRESENCE AS A WILLING VESSEL TO BE POURED OUT.

Don't hold back. Don't shut up the river that flows from My throne. Speak! Yes, speak but only at My direction, only the precious message given at the proper time.

WHAT YOU HEAR IN YOUR EAR, SPEAK!

Yes, I Am *That* Good

[*I was thinking about some things I sometimes say to the children that are not kind and feeling bad about it. I was contemplating how to change.*]

Don't worry about not sinning.

Just enter in.

Oh, My child, so many times in so many ways, I've revealed to you My heart, and yet you are slow to believe.

What is it about My grace that you can't accept?
What is it about My mercy that you can't believe?

Oh yes, I am *that* good!

Open up your heart to My leading. Resist no longer the promptings of My Spirit. Give heed to My step-by-step counsel.

Take heart, for you will see the change you desire.
You will *walk in that newness of Life*.[136]

You will reflect My Glory.

Shared by Laura Wilcott

My Jewel, Placed as I See Fit

Oh, don't be hesitant to believe all that I have said, for it will come to pass. Don't be one unable to grasp what you cannot see, for My Kingdom cannot be perceived without faith.

> *You are My jewel,[137] placed as I see fit, fashioned for My glory. I will perfect that which concerns you.[138]*

I AM the Molder of the clay.
I AM the Master Craftsman.
I determine the outcome, so be encouraged. Don't lose heart. I am molding you, even now, fashioning you as a precious jewel.

You will not be the same!

You will not follow this path for long. All will see the change I have wrought even now in your life.

Oh, be encouraged this day!

Woven for This Time in History

Take hold of that which I have laid out before you. Do not hold back. Do not question any longer the things I have for you, the things I have entrusted to you already, for they are a precious treasure, poured out for this time, not to be mishandled, not to be mislaid.

> **Take up the mantle placed before you.**
>
> **Take it up and put it on.**
>
> **Be, do, and go!**

Waste no time. It is time to enter the realm of My Spirit, to throw off *the works of the flesh.*[139] I will help you. I will guide you. I will hold your hand as you walk into the door set before you, so do not fear.

THE SPIRIT EXPRESSLY SAYS, "TAKE UP THE MANTLE I HAVE PLACED BEFORE YOU THIS DAY. WEAR IT WITH PRIDE, FOR YOUR FATHER CHOSE IT FOR YOU. IT HAS BEEN WOVEN FOR THIS HOUR, FOR THIS TIME IN HISTORY!"

GET OFF YOUR AGENDA

Let Me be what you cannot be.

Take refuge under My Wings. Seek My Face continually. Call on My Name.

I AM your Hiding Place.

RUN TO ME.

Cast your anxiety onto Me, for I do care for you.[140] I do anxiously await your call. But I am so much closer than that to you.

Walk in Me, through Me, by Me.

Don't wait so long. Acknowledge My Presence, moment by moment.

Your adversary has gained a foothold and must be thrust out. Expel him. He has no place. He is a defeated foe.

Don't give him a place.

Don't give him a voice.

To see the victory you desire, you must get off your agenda. You must stay in an attitude of worship. *You must enter that rest I have spoken of.*[141] *You must keep your mind stayed on Me.*

FOR THEN MY PEACE WILL BE THERE TO KEEP YOU.[142]

The Secret Things of My Kingdom

Move with Me! Glory in Me! Accept the mantle I have for you and move forward. Everything I've given you, all that I've entrusted to you, is for a season.

> My timing will prevail.
>
> My purposes will stand.

Only in Me will you know and perceive the timing of My Spirit. Be not enticed to follow or even entertain your thoughts. I will speak to your spirit the secret things of My Kingdom. You are but a vessel, being prepared for an hour, being washed out and filled up only to be poured out. See to it that you do not dismiss My gentle voice, My constant wooing, calling you to a better place—a place of rest.

You will see many things in the coming days. You will see many things come that will strike terror in the hearts of men. You must stand at attention as these events begin to take place, for I *will* to see you stand and walk. I *will* to see you rise up and take dominion over fear.[143] I *will* for you to stand in the face of this terror and rebuke it. I *will* for you to walk as one who walks on the clouds, for in My Kingdom, my subjects are not limited by time or space. They travel above the restrictions of this earth. They are sent on assignment and released at My Word. They speak; they do as I command. They offer up spiritual sacrifices in My Presence. They come at My command.

Shared by Laura Wilcott

Oh, that those who have been hand-picked for this hour would enter in and not hesitate, those called, those chosen to show forth My Glory and My Divine Power in these days. Enter in.

Oh, the time is ripe for those individuals who have been consecrated for the task at hand, to rise up and stand together as one. Yes, it is now, even now that I draw them together in spirit, that I knit their hearts as one.

Called Up, Sent Out

Do you love Me? Accept My instruction. Accept My discipline. Be moldable in My hands. Hold fast to that which I've given you.

It's expedient that you pay careful attention to My words, that you *draw near to Me*,[144] that you draw near to My sayings, for a time is coming when all will long for a refreshing word. You must be faithful to carry that word to those I send you.

Carry that word like a torch.

Don't look to the left or to the right. Fix your gaze directly before you. Keep to the path laid out for you.[145] Don't settle into complacency. Be on guard.

You will be called up.

You will be sent out.

You will be asked to stand for the many, to walk where they must walk, to carry that torch I give you. Rest in Me.

I will accomplish this, not you!

You, yes *you,* must carry what I tell you to those handpicked to hear, handpicked to receive My Glory, handpicked to walk in My river.

Handcrafted for My Glory

No vessel in a large house is without purpose, for each has its place and each its own function, some vessels for honor and others, dishonor.[146] You are of My house.

> I HAVE HANDCRAFTED YOU AS A VESSEL FOR MY GLORY.

I have hewn you out of the rock for this time. No one can say, "I know your place. I know your function," for I have not made it known, only to you.

Many will say in the coming days, weeks, months, and years, "You are this. You are that." But I say, don't pay any attention to them, for they do not seek My glory—only man's. They do not seek My interests—only theirs.

> FOR IF THEY SOUGHT MY GLORY, THEY WOULD NOT ELEVATE MAN. IF THEY SOUGHT MY APPROVAL, THEY WOULD NOT SEEK MAN'S.

Do not give them any notice. Just say, "I must work the works my Father has for me," for the work I have for you will not glorify man. To do the work I have for you, you must empty yourself completely.

> You must not hang on what they say.

My Kingdom is not a kingdom of titles.

Empowered for This Hour

In the coming days, you will see a work like no other you have seen before. For *I will pour out My Spirit*[147] on the thirsty, on those who have sought My will. They will walk by the way only to find themselves lacking, then I will come upon them, for My Spirit will not rest on the proud but the lowly. They will be pierced through to the heart only to find they are nothing, then My Spirit will rise within them.

My Spirit will rest upon the lowly, those who have not sought glory. I will come upon them in great glory! Needless to say, they will shine. My Glory will be round about them as they walk in the way, for many hardships await them. They will be empowered for this hour. They will be set in a place of harm but will be delivered by a mighty hand.

Only the righteous will dwell in a secure place. Only the prudent who walk uprightly will be satisfied with a drenching rain. The others will dwell in a parched, sun-scorched land for a time and a half a time. There will be no water. Their wells will be dry. They will wander, seeking a drink of water only to find their cup empty, while My faithful ones will be refreshed from the rivers of Life, so do not sit by as the wave begins to swell.

Drink in the Life-giving rains as you ride the wave of My Spirit. *For the Life-giving water* comes from above, but the force of the wave coming from beneath you is what will propel you. It is all My water.

Those who stand ashore, not venturing in early, will be swept away. They just come out to gape. They do not see it coming like a tidal wave. They will not stand, but those who are in the boat far out to sea will ride the wave without fear. Those standing on the shore have not heeded the warnings. They are blind. They are deaf, not giving heed to their actions, not walking circumspectly. Exhort the people!

Nothing Except Their Heart

Now is the time that those who are far off will see and those who are deaf will hear, for My Spirit is drawing them even now. They don't know why things have changed. They don't know what causes their thirst or what it is. They only know a gnawing at their spirit to enter into His rest—to come home. You must give attention to every detail of My plan, for many will long to come in. Many are rapping at the gate even now. Don't say of Me, "He wants this. He seeks that." Just hold their hand and help them in.

> I WANT NOTHING FROM THEM EXCEPT THEIR HEART.

I want to give to them all they are longing for. They seek peace. They seek love. They seek rest from their pain.

I want to fill them as I have you. I want to usher them into My Presence as I have you. I want to give them freedom from their bondage. I want to throw the shackles off their hands and their feet. Even now, those who wait at the gate are tired and hungry, tired of their lives longing for more, more of what they don't know.

Feed them. As I open the gate for them, one by one, as they pass by, take their hand and say, "Welcome home." I will make it plain who they are.

> ALL MY RICH BLESSING, ALL MY BOUNTY, ALL MY PROVISION IS STORED UP FOR THE MANY WHO WALK INTO MY ARMS.

Tender care has been given to bring them into the fold. Loving-kindness has been extended toward them.

Day by day, they come in. Make room for them. Set aside your heart for the task. You cannot say, "Peace, be still," to those outside the gate, only, "Come in," for there will be no peace for those who remain there. Even now, My fiery Presence is burning away the stony hearts from them, from those chosen to come in, and come in they will.

> From setting sun to setting sun, they will come in.

Only watch and see if I am not faithful to perform every word that I have said to you.

Take the Exit!

According to a predetermined plan have I laid out the events on the horizon. No, they won't come as a sunrise cresting ever so slowly. These events will come upon those who are haughty, vile, and right in their own eyes as a thief takes one by surprise, unaware one was lurking about until he is overcome. Oh, My child, be alert! Be watchful! Be circumspect!

To the many, it will seem as a dream of terror, a nightmare. Many will seek pleasure even as the signs are approaching, but they will be blinded to the warning signs. It's like one driving on a road with the bridge out and the sign warning of danger has been taken down.

Oh, so many will think they are on a safe road. So many travel with ease. They hurry along the highway, never giving thought to their ways. They have ignored My voice long enough. They have passed up all My exit signs. They have not given heed to My call; therefore, they will be left to travel *the road they've chosen*.[148]

My child, anchored are you to the Rock.[149] Yes, set securely. You shall not be moved. The waves will pound around you. The sea will roar. The vessels will crash at your side. No, unless one has learned to take shelter under My Wings, to abide in that safe place, they will be distraught and in anguish at what they see and hear. No, you are not to look with those eyes nor hear with those ears.

Handpicked for This Moment

Marked out for rebellion are those who have a haughty look and proud eyes. They do not seek to know My ways. They will have none of My sweet goodness, only misery and despair, for they constantly keep self on the throne. They exalt their weaknesses. They deny My strength. *They will be filled with the cup of My wrath for their stubborn and unrepentant hearts.*[150]

Watch and see My judgments come upon them speedily. Wait and discern My swift justice set in place. It is coming, and in that day, you will see My precious ones—those open to My voice, My leading, My calling—operating as I have enabled them: to be vessels of My Love.

> **Take your stand among those handpicked for the moment, those fashioned for this hour.**

Don't be timid.

Don't shrink back. Don't look to yourself to establish even the slightest change in course.

I have a set path for you and will cause you to stay the course, to adhere to the path. Now you must watch expectantly, waiting to see My Glory arise in this place, to see My little ones shine brightly.

As I Bear Them Up on My Wings

[I began to itch all over for no apparent reason. I asked the Lord, "Why am I itching?" The Lord answered,]

Like an itch that won't go away, like a nagging pain, like a speck in the eye, will it be as I begin to draw them. They will not be satisfied with their sin. They will not be able to rid themselves of any of it, yet they will long for relief.

Can't you see them coming? Can't you hear their shouts of joy as I throw off their burdens as I bear them up on My Wings! Yes! I can hear them! Oh, yes, I see them coming! Oh, what a day it will be!

"At last! At last!" they will cry. "At last, we have come home!" Oh, what a day it will be!

See! Don't you see it on the horizon? Myriads, myriads of wanderers seeking rest!

[I saw Jesus look toward the horizon where a myriad of people were coming toward Him. With His voice full of intense emotion, He cried,]

"Run out to greet them! Oh, run out to welcome them home! For the day has come for their return! The day has finally come for their rest! Rejoice! I say, rejoice! For My children have come home! *My children who were lost have come home to me!*[151] Oh, what a day!"

ENDNOTES

1. Isaiah 43:19 NIV
2. 2 Peter 1:18–19, NASV
3. Phillipians 3:14
4. Romans 12:1–2
5. Isaiah 30:21, NIV
6. Isaiah 41:10, NKJV
7. 1 Peter 4:11
8. Psalm 34:8
9. John 15:1
10. Hebrews 4:9–11
11. Numbers 22:9–20
12. Mark 4:23
13. Matthew 6:9–13
14. Isaiah 64:6
15. Psalm 119:105
16. 1 Peter 5:7
17. 2 Corinthians 10:4–5
18. Hosea 4:6
19. Matthew 11:28–29
20. James 4:7–8
21. 1 Corinthians 6:20
22. John 8:44
23. John 8:31–32, 36
24. Ephesians 6:16, NKJV
25. John 3:16
26. 1 Peter 1:18–19
27. 1 Peter 3:18
28. Jeremiah 17:9
29. Proverbs 29:25
30. John 8:31–32, 36
31. 2 Chronicles 16:9
32. Isaiah 40:31
33. Psalm 138:8

34 Isaiah 61:10
35 John 19:30
36 Exodus 3:14
37 1 Corinthians 6:20
38 Psalm 91
39 Matthew 4:35–41
40 Isaiah 63:9
41 Revelation 13:8
42 Isaiah 40:31, KJV
43 2 Timothy 2:20–21
44 Galatians 4:3–5, NASB
45 Isaiah 60:1, 2 Peter 1:19
46 Genesis 15:1
47 1 John 2:15–17
48 Matthew 11:27, NIV
49 Philippians 2:13
50 1 Peter 2:4–5
51 Jeremiah 29:11
52 Matthew 16:24
53 Isaiah 29:13
54 2 Corinthians 2:11
55 1 Peter 5:8
56 Psalm 46:1
57 1 John 4:18
58 *Lamentations 3:22–23*
59 Romans 5:5
60 Deuteronomy 31:6, 8
61 Deuteronomy 30:19
62 Psalm 8:2
63 Isaiah 45:5
64 Exodus 3:14
65 1 Peter 2:21
66 Psalm 91:1
67 Acts 3:1–16
68 Mark 10:46–52
69 Proverbs 3:5–6, NKJV

70   Isaiah 64:6
71   Matthew 11:28–30, NKJV
72   2 Corinthians 10:5
73   John 7:37
74   Mark 5:22–43
75   1 Peter 4:10–11
76   1 Samuel 15:22
77   Isaiah 61:10
78   Psalm 36:7–8
79   Isaiah 64:8
80   Psalm 12:8, NIV
81   Jeremiah 1:12
82   Exodus 3:14
83   Psalm 45:5
84   John 6:35
85   2 Corinthians 4:7, NIV
86   Romans 11:32–33
87   Matthew 11:28, NASB
88   Genesis 15:1
89   Matthew 26:39
90   Isaiah 60:1, NASB
91   John 15:1–11
92   John 17:20–23
93   1 Corinthians 10:1–4
94   Isaiah 26:3
95   John 15:1–8
96   John 14:6
97   Romans 5:17
98   Isaiah 30:15, Hebrews 4:9–11
99   1 John 2:20
100 Matthew 4:35–41
101 Isaiah 26:3
102 Zechariah 4:6
103 Isaiah 26:3
104 Philippians 4:8, NASB
105 John 14:27, NKJV

106   1 Corinthians 15:58, NKJV
107   Ephesians 6:13–17
108   John 9:41
109   Matthew 11:28–30
110   John 8:32, 36
111   Hebrews 12:2
112   Psalm 46:1
113   Philippians 3:10
114   1 Corinthians 15:57
115   Revelation 19:6
116   1 Corinthians 2:9
117   Hebrews 12:1-2
118   Isaiah 41:13
119   Psalm 91
120   1 Corinthians 10:1–4
121   Romans 6:13
122   Romans 9:23
123   Jeremiah 29:11–13
124   Matthew 3:12
125   John 10:27
126   Jude 1:24
127   Revelation 3:8
128   Hebrews 4:16
129   2 Timothy 2:20–21
130   Ephesians 6:13
131   Galatians 2:20
132   John 11:1–44
133   Romans 5:17
134   Psalm 149:5–9
135   John 8:12
136   Romans 6:1–4
137   Malachi 3:17, NKJV
138   Psalm 138:8, NKJV
139   Galatians 5:19–21
140   1 Peter 5:7
141   Matthew 11:28-30

142 Isaiah 26:3
143 2 Timothy 1:7
144 James 4:8
145 Proverbs 4:25–27
146 2 Timothy 2:20–21
147 Acts 2:17
148 Matthew 7:13–14
149 1 Corinthians 10:4
150 Romans 2:5
151 Luke 15:11–32

Printed in the USA
CPSIA information can be obtained
at www.ICGtesting.com
LVHW021928081024
793284LV00008B/288